FRACTIONS
Addition & Subtraction

Allan D. Suter

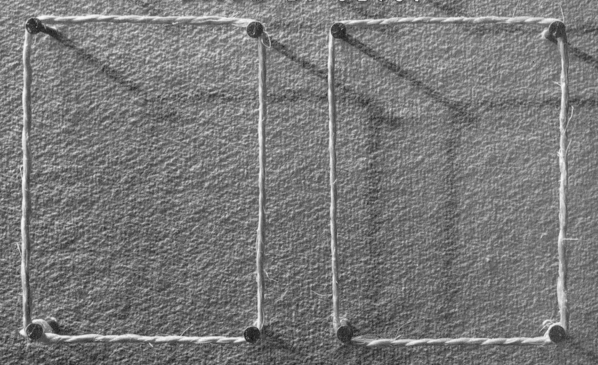

McGraw Hill **Contemporary**

Series Editor: Mitch Rosin
Executive Editor: Linda Kwil
Production Manager: Genevieve Kelley
Marketing Manager: Sean Klunder
Cover Design: Steve Strauss, ¡Think! Design

Send all inquiries to:
McGraw-Hill/Contemporary
130 East Randolph Street, Suite 400
Chicago, Illinois 60601

ISBN: 0-07-287109-1

Printed in the United States of America.

1 2 3 4 5 6 7 8 9 10   QPD/QPD   09 08 07 06 05 04 03

The **McGraw-Hill** Companies

■ Contents

Simplify each answer.

1. $\dfrac{4}{8} + \dfrac{3}{8} =$

Answer: _____

6. $5\dfrac{3}{8} + 2\dfrac{7}{16} =$

Answer: _____

2. Simplify $8\dfrac{7}{5}$.

Answer: _____

7.
$$\begin{array}{r} 2\dfrac{2}{3} \\[6pt] 5\dfrac{3}{4} \\[6pt] +\ 8\dfrac{1}{6} \\ \hline \end{array}$$

Answer: _____

3.
$$\begin{array}{r} 4\dfrac{5}{8} \\[6pt] +\ 9\dfrac{7}{8} \\ \hline \end{array}$$

Answer: _____

8.
$$\begin{array}{r} \dfrac{5}{6} \\[6pt] -\ \dfrac{1}{2} \\ \hline \end{array}$$

Answer: _____

4. What is the lowest common denominator for the fractions $\dfrac{1}{2}$ and $\dfrac{3}{5}$?

Answer: _____

9.
$$\begin{array}{r} 4\dfrac{2}{3} \\[6pt] -\ 1\dfrac{5}{12} \\ \hline \end{array}$$

Answer: _____

5.
$$\begin{array}{r} \dfrac{2}{3} \\[6pt] +\ \dfrac{1}{4} \\ \hline \end{array}$$

Answer: _____

10. The mixed number $5\dfrac{3}{8}$ is equal to 4 and how many eighths?

Answer: _____

11.

$$\begin{array}{r} 6 \\ -\ 2\frac{2}{3} \\ \hline \end{array}$$

Answer: _____

16. It took Mike $3\frac{1}{2}$ hours to mow Mrs. Yao's lawn and $1\frac{1}{4}$ hours to mow Mr. Miller's lawn. How much longer did it take to mow Mrs. Yao's lawn?

Answer: _____

12.

$$\begin{array}{r} 5\frac{1}{6} \\ +\ 2\frac{1}{3} \\ \hline \end{array}$$

Answer: _____

17. From a piece of cloth 6 yards long, Irma cut $4\frac{1}{2}$ yards to make a pair of curtains. How long was the remaining piece of cloth?

Answer: _____

13. $9\frac{7}{12} - 4\frac{1}{4} =$

Answer: _____

18. Jack ate $\frac{1}{3}$ of a pizza, and Janine ate $\frac{1}{6}$ of the pizza. Together, how much of the pizza did they eat?

Answer: _____

14. $8\frac{1}{5} - 7\frac{2}{3} =$

Answer: _____

19. Marlene's suitcase weighs $5\frac{3}{4}$ pounds. She packed $19\frac{7}{8}$ pounds of clothes. What is the combined weight of her suitcase and the clothes?

Answer: _____

15. Sal's bakery was open for $\frac{3}{4}$ of an hour on Sunday and $\frac{1}{2}$ hour on Monday. How many hours was the bakery open in all?

Answer: _____

20. Susana usually jogs 12 miles a week. By Thursday she had run $7\frac{3}{16}$ miles. How much farther does she have to run to reach her weekly goal?

Answer: _____

Evaluation Chart

On the following chart, circle the number of any problem you missed. The column after the problem number tells you the pages where those problems are taught. Based on your score, your teacher may ask you to study specific sections of this book. However, to thoroughly review your skills, begin with Unit 1 on page 7.

Skill Area	Pretest Problem Number	Skill Section	Review Page
Addition	1, 2, 3, 4, 5, 6, 7	7–30	18, 31, 57, 58
Subtraction	8, 9, 10, 11, 12, 13, 14	39–55	56, 57, 58
Addition Problem Solving	15, 18, 19	32–37	38, 66, 67
Subtraction Problem Solving	16, 17, 20	59–65	66, 67
Life-Skills Math	All	68–73	74

Compare and Add

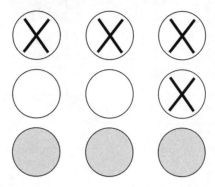

1. Compare the number of shaded circles to the total number of circles.

   Write the comparison as a fraction: $\dfrac{\boxed{}}{\boxed{9}}$ ←——— shaded circles

   ←——— total circles

2. Now compare the number of circles with an "X" inside to the total number of circles.

   Write the comparison as a fraction: $\dfrac{\boxed{}}{\boxed{}}$ ←——— circles with an "X"

   ←——— total circles

3. Combine the circles that are shaded with those that have an "X" inside. Compare that number to the total number of circles.

   Write the comparison as a fraction: $\dfrac{\boxed{}}{\boxed{}}$ ←——— circles with an "X" + shaded circles

   ←——— total circles

   This can be shown as an addition problem:

   $$\frac{3}{9} + \frac{4}{9} = \frac{7}{9}$$

Add the Fractions

In each problem, write the fractions and add them together.

1.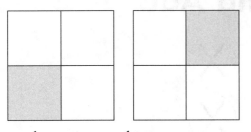

$$\underline{\dfrac{1}{4}} + \underline{\dfrac{1}{4}} = \underline{}$$
fraction shaded   fraction shaded   answer

4.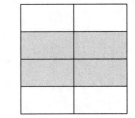

$$\underline{} + \underline{} = \underline{}$$
fraction shaded   fraction shaded   answer

2.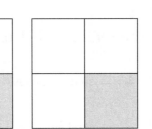

$$\underline{} + \underline{} = \underline{}$$
fraction shaded   fraction shaded   answer

5.

$$\underline{} + \underline{} = \underline{}$$
fraction shaded   fraction shaded   answer

3.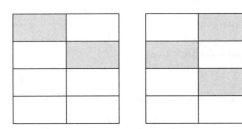

$$\underline{} + \underline{} = \underline{}$$
fraction shaded   fraction shaded   answer

6.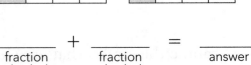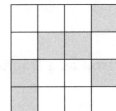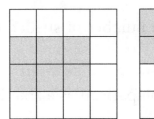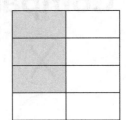

$$\underline{} + \underline{} = \underline{}$$
fraction shaded   fraction shaded   answer

> When adding fractions,
> - the denominators (bottom numbers) must be the same
> - only add the numerators (top numbers)

$$\frac{3}{5} + \frac{1}{5} = \frac{3+1}{5} = \frac{4}{5} \longleftarrow \text{numerator}$$
$$\phantom{\frac{3}{5} + \frac{1}{5} = \frac{3+1}{5} = \frac{4}{5}} \longleftarrow \text{denominator}$$

Like Denominators

When adding fractions, the denominators (bottom numbers) stay the same. Only the numerators (top numbers) are added.

EXAMPLE 1

$$\begin{array}{r} \dfrac{1}{5} \\[4pt] + \dfrac{2}{5} \\[4pt] \hline \dfrac{3}{5} \end{array}$$

$1 + 2 = 3$

EXAMPLE 2

$$\frac{3}{10} + \frac{4}{10} = \frac{3+4}{10} = \frac{7}{10}$$

Add the fractions.

1. $\begin{array}{r} \dfrac{4}{7} \\[4pt] + \dfrac{2}{7} \\[4pt] \hline \dfrac{\boxed{}}{\boxed{7}} \end{array}$

2. $\begin{array}{r} \dfrac{4}{14} \\[4pt] + \dfrac{7}{14} \\[4pt] \hline \dfrac{\boxed{}}{\boxed{}} \end{array}$

3. $\begin{array}{r} \dfrac{2}{6} \\[4pt] + \dfrac{3}{6} \\[4pt] \hline \dfrac{\boxed{}}{\boxed{}} \end{array}$

4. $\begin{array}{r} \dfrac{2}{11} \\[4pt] + \dfrac{7}{11} \\[4pt] \hline \dfrac{\boxed{}}{\boxed{11}} \end{array}$

5. $\begin{array}{r} \dfrac{9}{17} \\[4pt] + \dfrac{5}{17} \\[4pt] \hline \dfrac{\boxed{}}{\boxed{}} \end{array}$

6. $\begin{array}{r} \dfrac{6}{15} \\[4pt] + \dfrac{7}{15} \\[4pt] \hline \dfrac{\boxed{}}{\boxed{}} \end{array}$

7. $\dfrac{9}{15} + \dfrac{2}{15} = \dfrac{\boxed{}}{\boxed{15}}$

8. $\dfrac{4}{18} + \dfrac{7}{18} = \dfrac{\boxed{}}{\boxed{}}$

9. $\dfrac{1}{13} + \dfrac{2}{13} = \dfrac{\boxed{}}{\boxed{}}$

10. $\dfrac{7}{11} + \dfrac{2}{11} = \dfrac{\boxed{}}{\boxed{}}$

Add and Simplify

When adding fractions, sometimes you will need to **simplify** the answer.

$$\begin{array}{r} \frac{2}{6} \\[4pt] + \ \frac{2}{6} \\ \hline \frac{4}{6} \end{array} = \frac{2}{3}$$

$\frac{4}{6}$ can be **simplified,** or written in lower terms.

STEP 1

Find factors of 4 and 6.

4: 1, |2,| 4

6: 1, |2,| 3, 6

STEP 2

Divide by the greatest common factor.

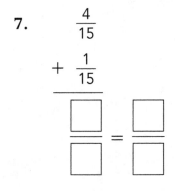

$$\frac{4}{6} \ \div \ \frac{2}{2} = \frac{2}{3}$$

1.
$$\begin{array}{r} \frac{1}{4} \\[4pt] + \ \frac{1}{4} \\ \hline \end{array}$$
$$\frac{\boxed{}}{\boxed{4}} = \frac{\boxed{}}{\boxed{2}}$$
simplified

2.
$$\begin{array}{r} \frac{3}{10} \\[4pt] + \ \frac{2}{10} \\ \hline \end{array}$$
$$\frac{\boxed{}}{\boxed{}} = \frac{\boxed{}}{\boxed{}}$$

3.
$$\begin{array}{r} \frac{3}{12} \\[4pt] + \ \frac{6}{12} \\ \hline \end{array}$$
$$\frac{\boxed{}}{\boxed{}} = \frac{\boxed{}}{\boxed{}}$$

4.
$$\begin{array}{r} \frac{3}{15} \\[4pt] + \ \frac{7}{15} \\ \hline \end{array}$$
$$\frac{\boxed{}}{\boxed{}} = \frac{\boxed{}}{\boxed{}}$$

5.
$$\begin{array}{r} \frac{7}{18} \\[4pt] + \ \frac{8}{18} \\ \hline \end{array}$$
$$\frac{\boxed{}}{\boxed{}} = \frac{\boxed{}}{\boxed{}}$$

6.
$$\begin{array}{r} \frac{8}{21} \\[4pt] + \ \frac{7}{21} \\ \hline \end{array}$$
$$\frac{\boxed{}}{\boxed{}} = \frac{\boxed{}}{\boxed{}}$$

7.
$$\begin{array}{r} \frac{4}{15} \\[4pt] + \ \frac{1}{15} \\ \hline \end{array}$$
$$\frac{\boxed{}}{\boxed{}} = \frac{\boxed{}}{\boxed{}}$$

8.
$$\begin{array}{r} \frac{4}{9} \\[4pt] + \ \frac{2}{9} \\ \hline \end{array}$$
$$\frac{\boxed{}}{\boxed{}} = \frac{\boxed{}}{\boxed{}}$$

9.
$$\begin{array}{r} \frac{10}{20} \\[4pt] + \ \frac{5}{20} \\ \hline \end{array}$$
$$\frac{\boxed{}}{\boxed{}} = \frac{\boxed{}}{\boxed{}}$$

Adding Mixed Numbers

Fractions and whole numbers can be combined to make **mixed numbers.**

Sometimes you will need to add mixed numbers.

Step 1: Add the fractions.

Step 2: Add the whole numbers.

Step 3: Simplify when necessary.

---

1. $5\frac{1}{9}$
   $+\ 7\frac{2}{9}$

   $12\frac{3}{9} = 12\frac{1}{3}$

5. $7\frac{5}{10}$
   $+\ 4\frac{4}{10}$

9. $6\frac{3}{10}$
   $+\ 15\frac{1}{10}$

2. $2\frac{2}{8}$
   $+\ 6\frac{4}{8}$

6. $3\frac{1}{4}$
   $+\ 4\frac{1}{4}$

10. $1\frac{2}{7}$
   $+\ 5\frac{3}{7}$

3. $2\frac{3}{8}$
   $+\ 9\frac{2}{8}$

7. $8\frac{3}{9}$
   $+\ 5\frac{4}{9}$

11. $12\frac{5}{16}$
   $+\ 13\frac{7}{16}$

4. $8\frac{5}{12}$
   $+\ 1\frac{1}{12}$

8. $3\frac{1}{6}$
   $+\ 7\frac{2}{6}$

12. $7\frac{3}{15}$
   $+\ 4\frac{5}{15}$

Fractions Greater Than 1

Some fractions, like $\frac{6}{6}$ or $\frac{9}{6}$, are equal to 1 or are larger than 1. These are called **improper fractions**.

Write the improper fraction and the mixed number for each picture.

1. $\dfrac{7}{4}$ = ☐ $\dfrac{☐}{☐}$

improper fraction   mixed number

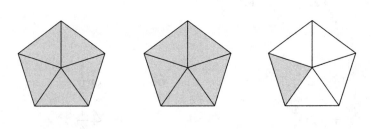

$\dfrac{4}{4}$ $\dfrac{3}{4}$

2. $\dfrac{☐}{5}$ = ☐ $\dfrac{☐}{☐}$

improper fraction   mixed number

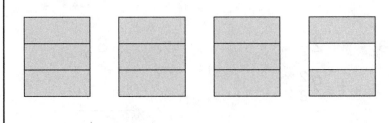

3. $\dfrac{☐}{☐}$ = ☐ $\dfrac{☐}{☐}$

improper fraction   mixed number

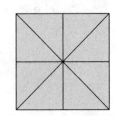 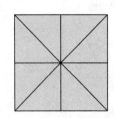 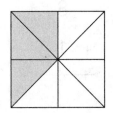

4. $\dfrac{☐}{☐}$ = ☐ $\dfrac{☐}{☐}$

improper fraction   mixed number

Change to Mixed Numbers

To change an improper fraction to a mixed number, divide the numerator by the denominator.

Change $\frac{8}{6}$ to a mixed number.

STEP 1
Write as a division problem.

$$\frac{8}{6} = \frac{8}{6\overline{)8}}$$

STEP 2
Divide. Write the remainder as a fraction. Simplify.

$$1\frac{2}{6} = 1\frac{1}{3}$$
$$\begin{array}{r} 1\frac{2}{6} \\ 6\overline{)8} \\ \underline{6} \\ 2 \end{array}$$

Change each improper fraction to a mixed number and simplify the remainder when necessary.

1. $\frac{10}{4} = 4\overline{)10}$

5. $\frac{21}{5} = 5\overline{)21}$

9. $\frac{11}{5} = 5\overline{)11}$

2. $\frac{7}{6} =$

6. $\frac{38}{6} =$

10. $\frac{57}{9} =$

3. $\frac{22}{6} =$

7. $\frac{7}{3} =$

11. $\frac{30}{5} =$

4. $\frac{9}{5} =$

8. $\frac{25}{10} =$

12. $\frac{15}{2} =$

Practice Simplifying

Sometimes the answer to an addition problem will contain an improper fraction. You cannot leave the answer in this form.

$$4\frac{3}{7}$$

$$+\quad 6\frac{5}{7}$$

$$10\frac{8}{7} = 11\frac{1}{7}$$

<u>STEP 1</u>

$$10\frac{8}{7} = 10 + \frac{8}{7}$$

$$\boxed{\frac{8}{7} = 1\frac{1}{7}}$$

<u>STEP 2</u>

$$10 + 1\frac{1}{7} = 11\frac{1}{7}$$

Change each improper fraction to a mixed number and add it to the whole number.

1. $2\frac{4}{3}$ = $\boxed{2}$ + $\dfrac{\boxed{4}}{\boxed{3}}$

   = $\boxed{2}$ + $\boxed{1}\dfrac{\boxed{1}}{\boxed{}}$

   = $\boxed{}\dfrac{\boxed{}}{\boxed{}}$

2. $5\frac{6}{5}$ = $\boxed{}$ + $\dfrac{\boxed{}}{\boxed{}}$

   = $\boxed{}$ + $\boxed{}\dfrac{\boxed{}}{\boxed{}}$

   = $\boxed{}\dfrac{\boxed{}}{\boxed{}}$

3. $6\frac{13}{8}$ = $\boxed{}$ + $\dfrac{\boxed{}}{\boxed{}}$

   = $\boxed{}$ + $\boxed{}\dfrac{\boxed{}}{\boxed{}}$

   = $\boxed{}\dfrac{\boxed{}}{\boxed{}}$

4. $11\frac{13}{6}$ = $\boxed{}$ + $\dfrac{\boxed{}}{\boxed{}}$

   = $\boxed{}$ + $\boxed{}\dfrac{\boxed{}}{\boxed{}}$

   = $\boxed{}\dfrac{\boxed{}}{\boxed{}}$

5. $8\frac{19}{9}$ = $\boxed{}$ + $\dfrac{\boxed{}}{\boxed{}}$

   = $\boxed{}$ + $\boxed{}\dfrac{\boxed{}}{\boxed{}}$

   = $\boxed{}\dfrac{\boxed{}}{\boxed{}}$

6. $7\frac{23}{8}$ = $\boxed{}$ + $\dfrac{\boxed{}}{\boxed{}}$

   = $\boxed{}$ + $\boxed{}\dfrac{\boxed{}}{\boxed{}}$

   = $\boxed{}\dfrac{\boxed{}}{\boxed{}}$

Simplify

Simplify each improper fraction to a mixed number and add it to the whole number.

1. $2\frac{11}{6} =$

2. $1\frac{17}{12} =$

3. $8\frac{11}{4} =$

4. $4\frac{3}{3} =$

5. $3\frac{5}{4} =$

6. $5\frac{15}{5} =$

7. $9\frac{9}{4} =$

8. $7\frac{12}{7} =$

9. $5\frac{10}{3} =$

10. $5\frac{13}{3} =$

11. $6\frac{5}{3} =$

12. $11\frac{16}{5} =$

13. $16\frac{3}{3} =$

14. $21\frac{5}{3} =$

15. $1\frac{9}{5} =$

16. $15\frac{13}{2} =$

17. $20\frac{14}{3} =$

18. $2\frac{9}{2} =$

Simplify Your Answers

Add the fractions and then simplify.

1.
$$\frac{4}{5}$$
$$+ \frac{3}{5}$$
$$\frac{\boxed{7}}{\boxed{5}} = \boxed{1}\frac{\boxed{2}}{\boxed{5}}$$

5.
$$\frac{5}{8}$$
$$+ \frac{7}{8}$$
$$\frac{\boxed{12}}{\boxed{8}} = \boxed{1}\frac{\boxed{4}}{\boxed{8}} = \boxed{1}\frac{\boxed{}}{\boxed{}}$$

2.
$$\frac{5}{7}$$
$$+ \frac{3}{7}$$
$$\frac{\boxed{}}{\boxed{}} = \boxed{}\frac{\boxed{}}{\boxed{}}$$

6.
$$\frac{5}{12}$$
$$+ \frac{11}{12}$$
$$\frac{\boxed{}}{\boxed{}} = \boxed{}\frac{\boxed{}}{\boxed{}} = \boxed{}\frac{\boxed{}}{\boxed{}}$$

3.
$$\frac{3}{4}$$
$$+ \frac{2}{4}$$
$$\frac{\boxed{}}{\boxed{}} = \boxed{}\frac{\boxed{}}{\boxed{}}$$

7.
$$\frac{8}{9}$$
$$+ \frac{4}{9}$$
$$\frac{\boxed{}}{\boxed{}} = \boxed{}\frac{\boxed{}}{\boxed{}} = \boxed{}\frac{\boxed{}}{\boxed{}}$$

4.
$$\frac{5}{6}$$
$$+ \frac{2}{6}$$
$$\frac{\boxed{}}{\boxed{}} = \boxed{}\frac{\boxed{}}{\boxed{}}$$

8.
$$\frac{7}{10}$$
$$+ \frac{5}{10}$$
$$\frac{\boxed{}}{\boxed{}} = \boxed{}\frac{\boxed{}}{\boxed{}} = \boxed{}\frac{\boxed{}}{\boxed{}}$$

Simplify When Necessary

Add the fractions and mixed numbers. Simplify when necessary.

1. $\dfrac{3}{8}$
$+ \ \dfrac{7}{8}$
_____

2. $1\dfrac{2}{9}$
$+ \ 5\dfrac{6}{9}$
_____

3. $\dfrac{5}{6}$
$+ \ \dfrac{4}{6}$
_____

4. $6\dfrac{1}{16}$
$+ \ \dfrac{3}{16}$
_____

5. $3\dfrac{7}{14}$
$+ \ 5\dfrac{3}{14}$
_____

6. $8\dfrac{1}{4}$
$+ \ 7$
_____

7. $4\dfrac{2}{11}$
$+ \ 9\dfrac{5}{11}$
_____

8. $1\dfrac{4}{15}$
$+ \ 3\dfrac{6}{15}$
_____

9. $\dfrac{7}{13}$
$+ \ \dfrac{8}{13}$
_____

10. $2\dfrac{1}{4}$
$+ \ 13\dfrac{3}{4}$
_____

11. $\dfrac{6}{7}$
$+ \ \dfrac{5}{7}$
_____

12. $3\dfrac{7}{10}$
$+ \ 5\dfrac{9}{10}$
_____

Addition Review

Add the fractions. Simplify when necessary.

1. $\dfrac{5}{13} + \dfrac{6}{13} =$

                        Answer: _____

6. $\dfrac{3}{8}$

      $+ \quad \dfrac{7}{8}$
      ‾‾‾‾‾‾

                        Answer: _____

2. $\dfrac{1}{15}$

   $+ \quad \dfrac{4}{15}$
   ‾‾‾‾‾‾

                        Answer: _____

7. $2\dfrac{2}{5}$

      $+ \quad 8\dfrac{3}{5}$
      ‾‾‾‾‾‾

                        Answer: _____

3. $4\dfrac{1}{3}$

   $+ \quad 2\dfrac{1}{3}$
   ‾‾‾‾‾‾

                        Answer: _____

8. $\dfrac{7}{10}$

      $+ \quad \dfrac{1}{10}$
      ‾‾‾‾‾‾

                        Answer: _____

4. $11\dfrac{8}{12}$

   $+ \quad 5\dfrac{5}{12}$
   ‾‾‾‾‾‾

                        Answer: _____

Change to a mixed number.

9. $\dfrac{13}{4} =$

                        Answer: _____

5. $\dfrac{2}{3}$

        $\dfrac{7}{3}$

   $+ \quad \dfrac{5}{3}$
   ‾‾‾‾‾‾

                        Answer: _____

Simplify.

10. $7\dfrac{13}{6} =$

                        Answer: _____

Multiples

When you multiply a whole number by 1, 2, 3, 4, and so on, the answers are called the **multiples** of the whole number.

5	5	5	5	5	5	5	5	5	5
× 1	× 2	× 3	× 4	× 5	× 6	× 7	× 8	× 9	×10
5	**10**	**15**	**20**	**25**	**30**	**35**	**40**	**45**	**50**

The multiples of 5 are: 5, 10, 15, 20, 25, 30, 35, 40, and so on.

Write the multiples of 8.

1.
8	8	8	8	8	8	8	8	8	8
× 1	× 2	× 3	× 4	× 5	× 6	× 7	× 8	× 9	×10
☐	☐	☐	☐	☐	☐	☐	☐	☐	☐

2. The first 10 multiples of 8 are: _____, _____, _____, _____, _____, _____,

_____, _____, _____, _____.

List the first 10 multiples of the following numbers:

3. 2: $\underset{\times 1}{2}$, $\underset{\times 2}{4}$, $\underset{\times 3}{6}$, $\underset{\times 4}{\rule{1cm}{0.4pt}}$, $\underset{\times 5}{\rule{1cm}{0.4pt}}$, $\underset{\times 6}{\rule{1cm}{0.4pt}}$, $\underset{\times 7}{\rule{1cm}{0.4pt}}$, $\underset{\times 8}{\rule{1cm}{0.4pt}}$, $\underset{\times 9}{\rule{1cm}{0.4pt}}$, $\underset{\times 10}{\rule{1cm}{0.4pt}}$

4. 3: 3, _____, _____, _____, _____, _____, _____, _____, _____, _____

5. 4: _____, _____, _____, _____, _____, _____, _____, _____, _____, _____

6. 6: _____, _____, _____, _____, _____, _____, _____, _____, _____, _____

7. 9: _____, _____, _____, _____, _____, _____, _____, _____, _____, _____

8. 12: _____, _____, _____, _____, _____, _____, _____, _____, _____, _____

Least Common Multiple

Find the least (smallest) common multiple (LCM) for 2 and 3.

List the first 10 multiples of 2:   2,   4,   6,   8,   10,   12,   14,   16,   18,   20

List the first 10 multiples of 3:   3,   6,   9,   12,   15,   18,   21,   24,   27,   30

The first 3 common multiples of 2 and 3 are: 6, 12, 18.

The **least common multiple** of 2 and 3 is: 6.

Write the multiples that are asked for in each problem.

1. List the first 10 multiples of 4: __4__, __8__, _____, _____, _____, _____,
   _____, _____, _____, _____

2. List the first 10 multiples of 6: __6__, _____, _____, _____, _____, _____,
   _____, _____, _____, _____

3. The first 3 common multiples of 4 and 6 are: _____, _____, _____

4. The least common multiple of 4 and 6 is: _____

---

5. List the first 10 multiples of 3: __3__, _____, _____, _____, _____, _____,
   _____, _____, _____, _____

6. List the first 10 multiples of 5: __5__, _____, _____, _____, _____, _____,
   _____, _____, _____, _____

7. The first 2 common multiples of 3 and 5 are: _____, _____

8. The least common multiple of 3 and 5 is: _____

---

9. List the first 10 multiples of 8: __8__, _____, _____, _____, _____, _____,
   _____, _____, _____, _____

10. List the first 10 multiples of 10: __10__, _____, _____, _____, _____, _____,
    _____, _____, _____, _____

11. The first 2 common multiples of 8 and 10 are: _____, _____

12. The least common multiple of 8 and 10 is: _____

Lowest Common Denominator

To add fractions that have different denominators, you will need to find the least common multiple. This will be the **lowest common denominator (LCD)**.

Finish the problems below. Find the multiples for the denominators.

1. $\frac{1}{4}$: $\underset{\times 1}{4}$, $\underset{\times 2}{\rule{1.5em}{0.4pt}}$, $\rule{1.5em}{0.4pt}$, $\rule{1.5em}{0.4pt}$, $\boxed{}$, $\rule{1.5em}{0.4pt}$, $\rule{1.5em}{0.4pt}$, 32

2. $\frac{1}{5}$: $\underset{\times 1}{5}$, $\underset{\times 2}{\rule{1.5em}{0.4pt}}$, $\rule{1.5em}{0.4pt}$, $\boxed{}$, $\rule{1.5em}{0.4pt}$, $\rule{1.5em}{0.4pt}$, $\rule{1.5em}{0.4pt}$, 40

3. Lowest common denominator of $\frac{1}{4}$ and $\frac{1}{5}$: $\rule{2em}{0.4pt}$

---

4. $\frac{5}{6}$: 6, $\rule{1.5em}{0.4pt}$, $\rule{1.5em}{0.4pt}$, $\rule{1.5em}{0.4pt}$, $\rule{1.5em}{0.4pt}$, $\rule{1.5em}{0.4pt}$, $\rule{1.5em}{0.4pt}$, $\rule{1.5em}{0.4pt}$

5. $\frac{3}{8}$: 8, $\rule{1.5em}{0.4pt}$, $\rule{1.5em}{0.4pt}$, $\rule{1.5em}{0.4pt}$, $\rule{1.5em}{0.4pt}$, $\rule{1.5em}{0.4pt}$, $\rule{1.5em}{0.4pt}$, $\rule{1.5em}{0.4pt}$

6. Lowest common denominator of $\frac{5}{6}$ and $\frac{3}{8}$: $\rule{2em}{0.4pt}$

---

7. $\frac{3}{7}$: 7, $\rule{1.5em}{0.4pt}$, $\rule{1.5em}{0.4pt}$, $\rule{1.5em}{0.4pt}$, $\rule{1.5em}{0.4pt}$, $\rule{1.5em}{0.4pt}$, $\rule{1.5em}{0.4pt}$, $\rule{1.5em}{0.4pt}$

8. $\frac{1}{4}$: 4, $\rule{1.5em}{0.4pt}$, $\rule{1.5em}{0.4pt}$, $\rule{1.5em}{0.4pt}$, $\rule{1.5em}{0.4pt}$, $\rule{1.5em}{0.4pt}$, $\rule{1.5em}{0.4pt}$, $\rule{1.5em}{0.4pt}$

9. Lowest common denominator of $\frac{3}{7}$ and $\frac{1}{4}$: $\rule{2em}{0.4pt}$

Find the Lowest Common Denominator (LCD)

Sometimes the lowest common denominator (LCD) is the larger of the two denominators.

This is true if the smaller denominator divides evenly into the larger denominator.

$$\frac{1}{3} + \frac{5}{18} \qquad 18 \div 3 = 6 \qquad \text{so, } 18 \text{ is the LCD.}$$

1. $\frac{3}{4}$ __4__, _____, _____
   multiples of 4

2. $\frac{7}{12}$ __12__, _____, _____
   multiples of 12

3. LCD of $\frac{3}{4}$ and $\frac{7}{12}$ _____

4. $\frac{5}{6}$ __6__, _____, _____
   multiples of 6

5. $\frac{2}{3}$ __3__, _____, _____
   multiples of 3

6. LCD of $\frac{5}{6}$ and $\frac{2}{3}$ _____

7. $\frac{1}{5}$ __5__, _____, _____
   multiples of 5

8. $\frac{3}{10}$ __10__, _____, _____
   multiples of 10

9. LCD of $\frac{1}{5}$ and $\frac{3}{10}$ _____

10. $\frac{5}{8}$ __8__, _____, _____, _____
    multiples of 8

11. $\frac{1}{2}$ __2__, _____, _____, _____
    multiples of 2

12. LCD of $\frac{5}{8}$ and $\frac{1}{2}$ _____

13. $\frac{1}{6}$ __6__, _____, _____
    multiples of 6

14. $\frac{1}{4}$ __4__, _____, _____
    multiples of 4

15. LCD of $\frac{1}{6}$ and $\frac{1}{4}$ _____

16. $\frac{2}{9}$ __9__, _____, _____
    multiples of 9

17. $\frac{2}{3}$ __3__, _____, _____
    multiples of 3

18. LCD of $\frac{2}{9}$ and $\frac{2}{3}$ _____

Choose the Best Method

$\dfrac{2}{7}$

$+ \dfrac{1}{14}$

Think:
Can you divide the denominators? Yes

$14 \div 7 = 2$
so 14 is the LCD.

$\dfrac{1}{3}$

$+ \dfrac{1}{2}$

Think:
What is the least common multiple?

3: 3, 6, 9, 12
2: 2, 4, 6, 8
The LCD is 6.

Find the lowest common denominator (LCD) for each pair of fractions. Choose Method 1 or Method 2.

1. $\dfrac{1}{8}$ $\dfrac{1}{3}$

   Method to use: __Method 2__

   LCD is __24__

2. $\dfrac{2}{3}$ $\dfrac{3}{5}$

   Method to use: _____

   LCD is _____

3. $\dfrac{3}{4}$ $\dfrac{5}{12}$

   Method to use: _____

   LCD is _____

4. $\dfrac{5}{6}$ $\dfrac{2}{9}$

   Method to use: _____

   LCD is _____

5. $\dfrac{2}{3}$ $\dfrac{5}{9}$

   Method to use: _____

   LCD is _____

6. $\dfrac{7}{11}$ $\dfrac{9}{22}$

   Method to use: _____

   LCD is _____

Fraction Readiness

Step 1: Use one of the methods on page 23 to find the lowest common denominator (LCD) for each pair of fractions.

Step 2: Change each pair of fractions to **like fractions** (fractions with the same denominator).

1. $\dfrac{2}{3} \times \boxed{\dfrac{2}{2}} = \dfrac{4}{6}$

    LCD = __6__

    $\dfrac{1}{2} \times \boxed{\dfrac{3}{3}} = \dfrac{3}{6}$

2. $\dfrac{2}{3} = \dfrac{\square}{12}$

    LCD = _____

    $\dfrac{3}{4} = \dfrac{\square}{12}$

3. $\dfrac{3}{5} = \dfrac{\square}{\square}$

    LCD = _____

    $\dfrac{7}{10} = \dfrac{\square}{\square}$

4. $\dfrac{8}{9} \times \boxed{\dfrac{2}{2}} = \dfrac{\square}{\square}$

    LCD = _____

    $\dfrac{5}{6} \times \boxed{\dfrac{3}{3}} = \dfrac{\square}{\square}$

5. $\dfrac{1}{4} = \dfrac{\square}{\square}$

    LCD = _____

    $\dfrac{5}{6} = \dfrac{\square}{\square}$

6. $\dfrac{5}{12} = \dfrac{\square}{\square}$

    LCD = _____

    $\dfrac{3}{8} = \dfrac{\square}{\square}$

7. $\dfrac{1}{2} = \dfrac{\square}{\square}$

    LCD = _____

    $\dfrac{1}{4} = \dfrac{\square}{\square}$

8. $\dfrac{1}{8} = \dfrac{\square}{\square}$

    LCD = _____

    $\dfrac{5}{6} = \dfrac{\square}{\square}$

Compare Unlike Fractions

Step 1: Find the lowest common denominator (LCD) for each pair of fractions.
Step 2: Change to like fractions (fractions with the same denominator).
Step 3: Compare using the symbols < (less than) or > (greater than).

1. $\dfrac{1}{3} = \dfrac{4}{12}$

2. $\dfrac{1}{4} = \dfrac{3}{12}$

3. $\dfrac{1}{3}$ ⟩ $\dfrac{1}{4}$

4. $\dfrac{1}{2} = \dfrac{\square}{\square}$

5. $\dfrac{5}{6} = \dfrac{\square}{\square}$

6. $\dfrac{1}{2}$ ◯ $\dfrac{5}{6}$

7. $\dfrac{2}{3} = \dfrac{\square}{\square}$

8. $\dfrac{4}{5} = \dfrac{\square}{\square}$

9. $\dfrac{2}{3}$ ◯ $\dfrac{4}{5}$

10. $\dfrac{5}{6} = \dfrac{\square}{\square}$

11. $\dfrac{2}{3} = \dfrac{\square}{\square}$

12. $\dfrac{5}{6}$ ◯ $\dfrac{2}{3}$

13. $\dfrac{3}{8} = \dfrac{\square}{\square}$

14. $\dfrac{3}{4} = \dfrac{\square}{\square}$

15. $\dfrac{3}{8}$ ◯ $\dfrac{3}{4}$

16. $\dfrac{1}{3} = \dfrac{\square}{\square}$

17. $\dfrac{3}{8} = \dfrac{\square}{\square}$

18. $\dfrac{1}{3}$ ◯ $\dfrac{3}{8}$

Compare Using Symbols

Step 1: Find the lowest common denominator (LCD) for each pair of fractions.

Step 2: Change to like fractions (fractions with the same denominator).

Step 3: Compare using the symbols < (less than) or > (greater than).

1. $\frac{2}{3}$ $\boxed{<}$ $\frac{4}{5}$

> Think:
>
> $\frac{2}{3} = \frac{10}{15}$ $\frac{4}{5} = \frac{12}{15}$

7. $\frac{7}{8}$ $\boxed{>}$ $\frac{3}{4}$

> Think:
>
> $\frac{7}{8} = \frac{7}{8}$ $\frac{3}{4} = \frac{6}{8}$

2. $\frac{5}{6}$ $\bigcirc$ $\frac{3}{4}$

8. $\frac{8}{15}$ $\bigcirc$ $\frac{2}{3}$

3. $\frac{2}{3}$ $\bigcirc$ $\frac{2}{5}$

9. $\frac{3}{4}$ $\bigcirc$ $\frac{2}{5}$

4. $\frac{4}{5}$ $\bigcirc$ $\frac{5}{6}$

10. $\frac{1}{4}$ $\bigcirc$ $\frac{3}{16}$

5. $\frac{1}{4}$ $\bigcirc$ $\frac{3}{8}$

11. $\frac{7}{10}$ $\bigcirc$ $\frac{4}{5}$

6. $\frac{7}{9}$ $\bigcirc$ $\frac{5}{6}$

12. $\frac{1}{2}$ $\bigcirc$ $\frac{4}{9}$

Adding with Unlike Denominators

Find the LCD and change to like fractions.

Add the numerators.

Simplify.

$$\frac{3}{4} \times \frac{3}{3} = \frac{9}{12}$$

$$+ \frac{2}{3} \times \frac{4}{4} = + \frac{8}{12}$$

$$\frac{3}{4} = \frac{9}{12}$$

$$+ \frac{2}{3} = + \frac{8}{12}$$

$$\frac{17}{12}$$

$$\frac{3}{4} = \frac{9}{12}$$

$$+ \frac{2}{3} = + \frac{8}{12}$$

$$\frac{17}{12} = 1\frac{5}{12}$$

Add the fractions. Simplify the answers when necessary.

1.
$$\frac{2}{3} = \underline{\quad}$$
$$+ \frac{1}{6} = + \underline{\quad}$$
$$\boxed{} \over \boxed{}$$

4.
$$\frac{5}{6}$$
$$+ \frac{3}{4}$$

7.
$$\frac{2}{3}$$
$$+ \frac{4}{7}$$

2.
$$\frac{3}{5} = \underline{\quad}$$
$$+ \frac{2}{10} = + \underline{\quad}$$
$$\frac{\boxed{}}{\boxed{}} = \frac{\boxed{}}{\boxed{}}$$

5.
$$\frac{2}{3}$$
$$+ \frac{1}{9}$$

8.
$$\frac{2}{3}$$
$$+ \frac{7}{12}$$

3.
$$\frac{1}{12} = \underline{\quad}$$
$$+ \frac{3}{4} = + \underline{\quad}$$
$$\frac{\boxed{}}{\boxed{}} = \frac{\boxed{}}{\boxed{}}$$

6.
$$\frac{3}{10}$$
$$+ \frac{1}{2}$$

9.
$$\frac{3}{4}$$
$$+ \frac{2}{5}$$

Unit 2 • Lowest Common Denominator

Adding Mixed Numbers with Unlike Denominators

Step 1: Change to like fractions.
Step 2: Add the whole numbers and the fractions.
Step 3: Simplify if necessary.

$$7\frac{1}{2} = 7\frac{4}{8}$$
$$+\ 8\frac{3}{4} = +\ 8\frac{6}{8}$$

change to like fractions

$$15\frac{10}{8} = 16\frac{2}{8} = 16\frac{1}{4}$$

add the mixed numbers

simplify if necessary

Add the mixed numbers. Simplify if necessary.

1. $7\frac{1}{5} = \ 7\text{—}$

   $+\ 3\frac{2}{3} = +3\text{—}$

4. $4\frac{3}{10}$

   $+\ 2\frac{1}{5}$

7. $1\frac{3}{7}$

   $+\ 3\frac{1}{2}$

2. $2\frac{1}{2} = \ 2\text{—}$

   $+\ 5\frac{2}{3} = +5\text{—}$

5. $6\frac{7}{12}$

   $+\ 9\frac{2}{3}$

8. $16\frac{7}{10}$

   $+\ 3\frac{1}{2}$

3. $3\frac{11}{12} = \ 3\text{—}$

   $+\ 4\frac{3}{4} = +4\text{—}$

6. $3\frac{2}{5}$

   $+\ 6\frac{1}{4}$

9. $18\frac{5}{12}$

   $+\ 10\frac{1}{4}$

Mixed Practice

Add the fractions and mixed numbers. Simplify answers when necessary.

1. $\begin{array}{r} \frac{5}{12} \\ + \frac{1}{8} \\ \hline \end{array}$

2. $\begin{array}{r} 4\frac{3}{14} \\ + 5\frac{2}{7} \\ \hline \end{array}$

3. $\begin{array}{r} 8\frac{5}{8} \\ + 3\frac{2}{3} \\ \hline \end{array}$

4. $\begin{array}{r} 7\frac{2}{3} \\ + 9\frac{8}{15} \\ \hline \end{array}$

5. $\begin{array}{r} 12\frac{1}{2} \\ + 16\frac{3}{10} \\ \hline \end{array}$

6. $\begin{array}{r} 24\frac{2}{3} \\ + 8\frac{5}{6} \\ \hline \end{array}$

7. $\begin{array}{r} \frac{3}{4} \\ + \frac{5}{6} \\ \hline \end{array}$

8. $\begin{array}{r} 20\frac{2}{3} \\ + 17\frac{1}{6} \\ \hline \end{array}$

9. $\begin{array}{r} 16\frac{3}{4} \\ + 9\frac{11}{12} \\ \hline \end{array}$

10. $\begin{array}{r} 18\frac{7}{9} \\ + 11\frac{5}{6} \\ \hline \end{array}$

11. $\begin{array}{r} 2\frac{1}{4} \\ + 6\frac{5}{12} \\ \hline \end{array}$

12. $\begin{array}{r} 13\frac{11}{24} \\ + 28\frac{7}{8} \\ \hline \end{array}$

Adding Three Numbers

To add three or more fractions:

$$\frac{1}{2} = \frac{6}{12}$$

$$\frac{2}{3} = \frac{8}{12}$$

$$+ \frac{3}{4} = + \frac{9}{12}$$

$$\frac{23}{12} = 1\frac{11}{12}$$

Step 1: Find the least common multiple of the denominators.

2: 2, 4, 6, 8, 10, $\boxed{12}$

3: 3, 6, 9, $\boxed{12}$

4: 4, 8, $\boxed{12}$

Step 2: Change to like fractions.

Step 3: Add and simplify when necessary.

1.
$$3\frac{1}{4} = 3\frac{}{8}$$
$$1\frac{1}{8} = 1\frac{}{8}$$
$$+ \; 5\frac{1}{2} = 5\frac{}{8}$$
$$9\frac{}{8}$$

4.
$$\frac{2}{3}$$
$$\frac{1}{6}$$
$$+ \; \frac{5}{12}$$

7.
$$9\frac{1}{2}$$
$$7\frac{1}{4}$$
$$+ \; 2\frac{7}{8}$$

2.
$$\frac{7}{10}$$
$$\frac{3}{5}$$
$$+ \; \frac{1}{2}$$

5.
$$8\frac{2}{3}$$
$$4\frac{1}{5}$$
$$+ \; 5\frac{1}{3}$$

8.
$$1\frac{1}{6}$$
$$6\frac{1}{4}$$
$$+ \; 7\frac{1}{3}$$

3.
$$4\frac{2}{3}$$
$$6\frac{3}{8}$$
$$+ \; 2\frac{1}{4}$$

6.
$$\frac{4}{9}$$
$$\frac{1}{6}$$
$$+ \; \frac{2}{3}$$

9.
$$3\frac{1}{4}$$
$$1\frac{4}{5}$$
$$+ \; 5\frac{1}{2}$$

Lowest Common Denominator Review

1. List the first six multiples of 4.

————, ————, ————,

————, ————, ————

2. List the first six multiples of 6.

————, ————, ————,

————, ————, ————

3. What is the least common multiple of 4 and 6?

Answer: _____

4. What is the lowest common denominator of $\frac{3}{4}$ and $\frac{1}{2}$?

Answer: _____

5. What is the LCD of $\frac{2}{9}$ and $\frac{5}{6}$?

Answer: _____

6. Compare the fractions using <, >, or =.

$\frac{1}{4}$ ◯ $\frac{2}{5}$

7. Compare the fractions using <, >, or =.

$\frac{8}{10}$ ◯ $\frac{3}{5}$

8. Add. Simplify if necessary.

$$1\frac{3}{7}$$
$$+\ \ 3\frac{1}{2}$$

Answer: _____

9. Add. Simplify if necessary.

$$18\frac{2}{3}$$
$$+\ \ 8\frac{5}{6}$$

Answer: _____

10. Add. Simplify if necessary.

$$8\frac{2}{3}$$
$$4\frac{1}{4}$$
$$+\ \ 5\frac{1}{3}$$

Answer: _____

Does the Answer Make Sense?

Write a number sentence for each problem below. Then write the answer in the sentence below the problem. Read it and ask yourself, "Does the answer make sense?"

1. Angelia bought $4\frac{5}{8}$ pounds of grapefruit and $7\frac{1}{3}$ pounds of apples. How many pounds of fruit did she buy altogether?

   $$\underline{\quad 4\frac{5}{8} \quad} \quad \underline{\quad + \quad} \quad \underline{\quad 7\frac{1}{3} \quad} \quad = \quad \underline{\qquad}$$
   number   operation   number   answer
            symbol

   Angelia bought _____ pounds of fruit altogether.

2. Janetta worked $6\frac{1}{2}$ hours of overtime last week and $3\frac{1}{4}$ hours this week. How many hours of overtime did she work?

   $$\underline{\qquad} \quad \underline{\qquad} \quad \underline{\qquad} \quad = \quad \underline{\qquad}$$
   number   operation   number   answer
            symbol

   Janetta worked _____ hours of overtime.

3. Mark needs $1\frac{1}{2}$ cups of chopped nuts for the batter and $\frac{3}{4}$ cup chopped nuts for the frosting. How many cups of chopped nuts does he need altogether?

   $$\underline{\qquad} \quad \underline{\qquad} \quad \underline{\qquad} \quad = \quad \underline{\qquad}$$
   number   operation   number   answer
            symbol

   Mark needs _____ cups of chopped nuts altogether.

4. Adrian bought $5\frac{3}{4}$ gallons of gas on Wednesday and $12\frac{1}{2}$ gallons on Saturday. How many gallons of gas did he buy in all?

   $$\underline{\qquad} \quad \underline{\qquad} \quad \underline{\qquad} \quad = \quad \underline{\qquad}$$
   number   operation   number   answer
            symbol

   Adrian bought _____ gallons in all.

5. Johanna bought $1\frac{5}{8}$ pounds of candy and $2\frac{3}{4}$ pounds of peanuts. How many pounds of candy and peanuts did she buy?

   $$\underline{\qquad} \quad \underline{\qquad} \quad \underline{\qquad} \quad = \quad \underline{\qquad}$$
   number   operation   number   answer
            symbol

   Johanna bought _____ pounds of peanuts and candy.

6. Kim's shampoo usually comes in an $8\frac{1}{2}$-ounce bottle. This week she bought a bottle with a $2\frac{1}{2}$-ounce bonus. How much shampoo did she get altogether?

   $$\underline{\qquad} \quad \underline{\qquad} \quad \underline{\qquad} \quad = \quad \underline{\qquad}$$
   number   operation   number   answer
            symbol

   Kim got _____ ounces of shampoo.

Number Sentences

Write a number sentence for each problem below. Then write the answer in the sentence below the problem. Read it and ask yourself, "Does the answer make sense?"

1. The shop opened for $\frac{3}{4}$ of an hour on Monday and $\frac{1}{2}$ of an hour on Tuesday. How many hours was the shop open in all?

   _____ _____ _____ = _____
   number   operation   number   answer
            symbol

   The shop was open for _____ hours in all.

4. Joe worked out $1\frac{1}{2}$ hours on Thursday and then increased his workout by $\frac{1}{4}$ of an hour on Friday. How long was his workout on Friday?

   _____ _____ _____ = _____
   number   operation   number   answer
            symbol

   Joe's workout on Friday was _____ hours long.

2. Sue has a book report due next week. She read $\frac{1}{3}$ of the book last week and $\frac{1}{4}$ this week. How much has she read so far?

   _____ _____ _____ = _____
   number   operation   number   answer
            symbol

   Sue has read _____ of the book.

5. Mr. Miller took a trip and drove $\frac{3}{5}$ of the way on the first day and $\frac{1}{5}$ of the way on the second day. What portion of the trip did he drive in the 2 days?

   _____ _____ _____ = _____
   number   operation   number   answer
            symbol

   Mr. Miller drove _____ of the trip in 2 days.

3. Patti spent $1\frac{3}{4}$ hours practicing tennis and $2\frac{1}{2}$ hours on homework. How much time did she spend practicing tennis and doing homework?

   _____ _____ _____ = _____
   number   operation   number   answer
            symbol

   Patti spent _____ hours practicing tennis and doing homework.

6. The recipe called for cutting up $\frac{1}{3}$ of a pound of strawberries and $\frac{1}{5}$ of pound of cherries. What part of a pound was cut up altogether?

   _____ _____ _____ = _____
   number   operation   number   answer
            symbol

   Altogether, _____ of a pound was cut up.

Picture Problems

Use the drawings to help solve the problems.

1.

John bought $3\frac{1}{2}$ pounds of grapes. He also bought $2\frac{1}{2}$ pounds of bananas. How much fruit did John buy?

Answer: _____

4.

The cookie recipe needs $\frac{3}{4}$ cup of sugar and $\frac{1}{3}$ cup brown sugar. How much sugar is used in all?

Answer: _____

2.

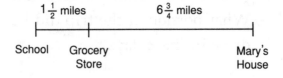

What is the distance from the school to Mary's house?

Answer: _____

5.

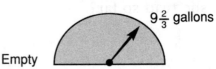

If Tina adds $3\frac{3}{4}$ gallons to her gas tank, how much gas will she have?

Answer: _____

3.

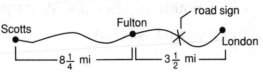

How far is it from Scotts to London?

Answer: _____

6.

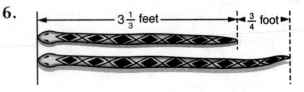

How long are both snakes together?

Answer: _____

Using Symbols

NUMBER RELATION SYMBOLS

$<$ is less than
$>$ is greater than
$=$ is equal to
$\neq$ is not equal to

Amanda ran $4\frac{1}{3}$ miles on Saturday and $3\frac{3}{4}$ miles on Sunday. Using these facts, fill in the blanks below.

1. Amanda ran farther on Saturday than on Sunday.

$$4\frac{1}{3}$$
_____ _____ _____
Saturday   symbol   Sunday

2. How far did Amanda run altogether?

_____ $+$ $3\frac{3}{4}$ $=$ _____
Saturday   Sunday   answer

3. Amanda ran less on Sunday than on Saturday.

$$3\frac{3}{4}$$
_____ _____ _____
Sunday   symbol   Saturday

4. Amanda did not run the same distance on both days.

_____ _____ _____
Saturday   symbol   Sunday

Randy used $7\frac{5}{8}$ yards of fabric to make curtains. He used $2\frac{1}{4}$ yards of fabric to make a tablecloth. Using these facts, fill in the blanks below.

5. Randy used more fabric to make the curtains than to make the tablecloth.

$$7\frac{5}{8}$$
_____ _____ _____
curtains   symbol   tablecloth

6. How much fabric did Randy use altogether?

_____ $+$ $2\frac{1}{4}$ $=$ _____
curtains   tablecloth   answer

7. Randy used less fabric to make the tablecloth than to make the curtains.

$$2\frac{1}{4}$$
_____ _____ _____
tablecloth   symbol   curtains

8. Randy did not use the same amount of fabric.

_____ _____ _____
curtains   symbol   tablecloth

Write a Question

To add properly, you must read carefully. One way to learn to read carefully is to write your own questions.

1. Two pieces of wood measure $9\frac{3}{8}$ and $4\frac{3}{4}$ feet.

   Write a question about the facts if the answer is $14\frac{1}{8}$.

   _____

   _____

2. Zelda bought $2\frac{1}{3}$ pounds of chocolate, $3\frac{2}{5}$ pounds of peanuts, and $1\frac{2}{3}$ pounds of hard candy.

   Write a question about the facts if the answer is:

   a) 4 pounds _____

   _____

   _____

   b) $7\frac{2}{5}$ pounds _____

   _____

   c) $5\frac{1}{15}$ pounds _____

   _____

   _____

3. The trip takes $\frac{1}{2}$ hour by car, $2\frac{3}{4}$ hours by plane, and $1\frac{1}{2}$ hours by bus.

   Write a question about the facts if the answer is:

   a) $4\frac{3}{4}$ hours _____

   _____

   b) $3\frac{1}{4}$ hours _____

   _____

4. Carol is $60\frac{3}{4}$ inches tall. Marc is $71\frac{3}{8}$ inches tall.

   Write a question about the facts if the answer is $132\frac{1}{8}$ inches.

   _____

   _____

5. Matilda drove $5\frac{1}{2}$ miles, Cloe drove $3\frac{7}{8}$ miles, and Amy drove $7\frac{3}{4}$ miles.

   Write a question about the facts if the answer is:

   a) $17\frac{1}{8}$ miles _____

   _____

   b) $9\frac{3}{8}$ miles _____

   _____

   b) $11\frac{5}{8}$ miles _____

   _____

6. Juan drew a line that measured $4\frac{5}{6}$ inches. Then he drew a line that measured $3\frac{3}{4}$ inches.

   Write a question about the facts if the answer is $8\frac{7}{12}$ inches.

   _____

   _____

Addition Word Problems

Write a number sentence for each problem below. Then write the answer in the sentence below the problem. Read it and ask yourself, "Does the answer make sense?"

1. Emily has $3\frac{1}{2}$ yards of fabric. She bought another $1\frac{2}{3}$ yards. How much fabric does she have?

   _____ _____ _____ = _____
   number operation number   answer
            symbol

   Emily has _____ yards of fabric.

2. Matteo took a nap for $\frac{3}{4}$ of an hour on Monday. He took another nap for $\frac{1}{2}$ an hour on Tuesday. How long did he nap in total?

   _____ _____ _____ = _____
   number operation number   answer
            symbol

   Matteo napped for _____ hours.

3. San Juan received $2\frac{1}{4}$ inches of rain on Friday. On Saturday it rained $\frac{3}{4}$ inches. How much rain did the city receive on both days?

   _____ _____ _____ = _____
   number operation number   answer
            symbol

   It rained _____ inches in San Juan.

4. Sandra bought $3\frac{1}{2}$ pounds of roast beef and $2\frac{1}{8}$ pounds of turkey. How much did she buy in all?

   _____ _____ _____ = _____
   number operation number   answer
            symbol

   Sandra bought _____ pounds.

5. The restaurant used $5\frac{1}{4}$ gallons of milk and $1\frac{2}{3}$ gallons of cream. How many gallons did the restaurant use altogether?

   _____ _____ _____ = _____
   number operation number   answer
            symbol

   The restaurant used _____ gallons.

6. Mike drove $23\frac{3}{8}$ miles to work. Then he drove $15\frac{3}{4}$ miles to see his friends. How far did he drive in all?

   _____ _____ _____ = _____
   number operation number   answer
            symbol

   Mike drove _____ miles in all.

Addition Problem-Solving Review

1. Kendra's dishwashing soap comes in a $14\frac{3}{4}$-ounce bottle. This week she bought a bottle with an additional $3\frac{1}{3}$ ounces. How much soap did she buy?

   _____ _____ _____ = _____
   number operation number   answer
            symbol

   Answer: _____

2. Jenna worked $34\frac{1}{2}$ hours this week and $38\frac{3}{4}$ hours last week. How many hours did she work during both weeks?

   _____ _____ _____ = _____
   number operation number   answer
            symbol

   Answer: _____

3. Tracy typed $20\frac{1}{4}$ pages of text during her first hour at work. During her second hour she typed $25\frac{1}{2}$ pages. How many pages did she type in all?

   _____ _____ _____ = _____
   number operation number   answer
            symbol

   Answer: _____

4. Tynen was given $3\frac{1}{2}$ packs of baseball cards. His sister gave him an additional $5\frac{3}{4}$ packs. How many packs of cards does Tynen have?

   _____ _____ _____ = _____
   number operation number   answer
            symbol

   Answer: _____

5.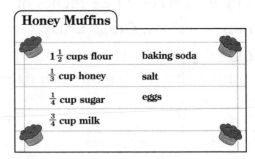

   Tori bought two cartons of eggs. One carton contained $\frac{12}{12}$ usable eggs, while the other carton contained $\frac{4}{12}$ usable eggs. What fraction of the eggs were usable? Simplify if necessary.

   Answer: _____

6.

Honey Muffins	
$1\frac{1}{2}$ cups flour	baking soda
$\frac{1}{3}$ cup honey	salt
$\frac{1}{4}$ cup sugar	eggs
$\frac{3}{4}$ cup milk	

   How many total cups of ingredients are in the muffins?

   Answer: _____

How Much Is Left?

Use the drawings to help solve the subtraction problems. Find the fraction labeled "start." Then count the number of fractions to "stop." Subtract.

1. $\dfrac{4}{5} - \dfrac{3}{5} = \dfrac{\square}{5}$ ←—— numerator

←—— denominator

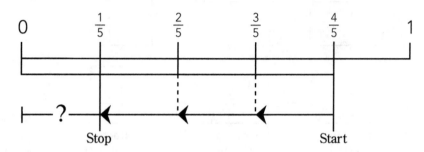

2. $\dfrac{7}{10} - \dfrac{4}{10} =$ _____
answer

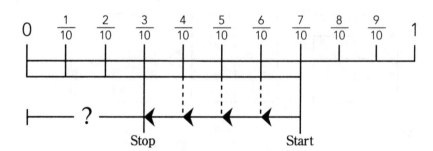

3. $\dfrac{5}{6} - \dfrac{4}{6} =$ _____
answer

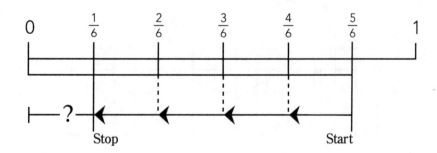

4. It's easy. When the denominators are the same, you just

__S__ __ __B__ __ __ __ __ __ __T__ the numerators.
word

Take Away the Fractions

When the bottom numbers (denominators) are the same, you just subtract the top numbers (numerators).

Complete the subtraction problems using the drawings.

1.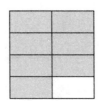

$$\frac{3}{4} \quad - \quad \frac{2}{4} \quad = \quad \frac{\square}{4}$$

fraction shaded   fraction shaded   fraction shaded

2.

$$- \qquad\qquad =$$

fraction shaded   fraction shaded   fraction shaded

3.

$$- \qquad\qquad =$$

fraction shaded   fraction shaded   fraction shaded

Subtracting with Like Denominators

When subtracting fractions, the denominators must be the same. Only the numerators are subtracted.

Subtract the fractions. Simplify your answers when necessary.

1. $\dfrac{5}{7}$
   $-\dfrac{2}{7}$
   _____
   $\dfrac{3}{7}$
   $5 - 2 = 3$

5. $\dfrac{13}{15}$
   $-\dfrac{3}{15}$
   _____
   $13 - 3 = 10$

9. $\dfrac{4}{6}$
   $-\dfrac{3}{6}$
   _____
   $4 - 3 = 1$

2. $\dfrac{7}{10}$
   $-\dfrac{1}{10}$
   _____

6. $\dfrac{15}{21}$
   $-\dfrac{6}{21}$
   _____

10. $\dfrac{9}{11}$
    $-\dfrac{3}{11}$
    _____

3. $\dfrac{3}{8}$
   $-\dfrac{1}{8}$
   _____

7. $\dfrac{4}{5}$
   $-\dfrac{1}{5}$
   _____

11. $\dfrac{13}{15}$
    $-\dfrac{1}{15}$
    _____

4. $\dfrac{9}{10}$
   $-\dfrac{5}{10}$
   _____

8. $\dfrac{3}{4}$
   $-\dfrac{1}{4}$
   _____

12. $\dfrac{6}{7}$
    $-\dfrac{1}{7}$
    _____

Subtracting Mixed Numbers

When subtracting **mixed numbers** with fractions that have the same denominators:

Step 1: Subtract the fractions.
Step 2: Subtract the whole numbers.
Step 3: Simplify when necessary.

---

1. $5\frac{4}{5}$
$-\ 3\frac{1}{5}$

$2\frac{\boxed{}}{5}$

5. $7\frac{7}{8}$
$-\ 3\frac{3}{8}$

$4\frac{\boxed{}}{8} = 4\frac{\boxed{}}{2}$

9. $11\frac{9}{10}$
$-\ 5\frac{3}{10}$

$6\frac{\boxed{}}{10} = 6\frac{\boxed{}}{5}$

2. $7\frac{8}{9}$
$-\ 2\frac{5}{9}$

6. $8\frac{11}{15}$
$-\ 5\frac{2}{15}$

10. $12\frac{15}{16}$
$-\ 4\frac{1}{16}$

3. $15\frac{5}{6}$
$-\ 8\frac{1}{6}$

7. $9\frac{17}{24}$
$-\ 4\frac{5}{24}$

11. $8\frac{6}{11}$
$-\ 2\frac{4}{11}$

4. $4\frac{6}{8}$
$-\ 1\frac{1}{8}$

8. $12\frac{16}{20}$
$-\ 3\frac{13}{20}$

12. $17\frac{9}{15}$
$-\ 7\frac{6}{15}$

Subtracting Fractions with Unlike Denominators

STEP 1

Find the LCD and change to like fractions.

$$\frac{3}{5} \times \boxed{\frac{2}{2}} = \frac{6}{10}$$

$$-\frac{1}{10} \times \boxed{\frac{1}{1}} = -\frac{1}{10}$$

STEP 2

Subtract the numerators.

$$\frac{3}{5} = \frac{6}{10}$$

$$-\frac{1}{10} = -\frac{1}{10}$$

$$\frac{5}{10}$$

STEP 3

Simplify.

$$\frac{3}{5} = \frac{6}{10}$$

$$-\frac{1}{10} = -\frac{1}{10}$$

$$\frac{5}{10} = \frac{1}{2}$$

Subtract the fractions. Simplify your answers when necessary.

1.
$$\frac{2}{3} \times \boxed{\frac{5}{5}} = \frac{10}{15}$$
$$-\frac{3}{5} \times \boxed{\frac{3}{3}} = -\frac{9}{15}$$
$$\frac{1}{15}$$

4.
$$\frac{3}{4}$$
$$-\frac{5}{12}$$

7.
$$\frac{7}{8}$$
$$-\frac{3}{4}$$

2.
$$\frac{3}{4} = \underline{\quad}$$
$$-\frac{2}{3} = \underline{\quad}$$
$$\underline{\quad}$$

5.
$$\frac{5}{9}$$
$$-\frac{1}{3}$$

8.
$$\frac{4}{5}$$
$$-\frac{3}{10}$$

3.
$$\frac{5}{6} = \underline{\quad}$$
$$-\frac{1}{3} = \underline{\quad}$$
$$\underline{\quad} = \underline{\quad}$$

6.
$$\frac{5}{6}$$
$$-\frac{1}{9}$$

9.
$$\frac{5}{6}$$
$$-\frac{1}{12}$$

Subtracting Mixed Numbers with Unlike Denominators

Step 1: Find the lowest common denominator and change to like fractions.

Step 2: Subtract the fractions and the whole numbers.

Step 3: Simplify when necessary.

$$9\frac{3}{4} = 9\frac{9}{12}$$
$$- 5\frac{1}{6} = - 5\frac{2}{12}$$

change to like fractions

$$4\frac{7}{12}$$

subtract fractions first

---

1. $7\frac{9}{10} = 7\text{---}$

   $- 3\frac{1}{2} = - 3\text{---}$

4. $7\frac{5}{6}$

   $- 3$ ←no fraction

   $\frac{5}{6}$ ←bring down the fraction

7. $3\frac{3}{4}$

   $- 1\frac{5}{12}$

2. $8\frac{3}{5} = 8\text{---}$

   $- 1\frac{1}{10} = - 1\text{---}$

5. $9\frac{2}{3}$

   $- 7\frac{3}{5}$

8. $7\frac{5}{6}$

   $- 3\frac{1}{2}$

3. $6\frac{2}{3} = 6\text{---}$

   $- 2\frac{1}{4} = - 2\text{---}$

6. $4\frac{9}{10}$

   $- 1\frac{2}{5}$

9. $9\frac{3}{5}$

   $- 3$

Subtraction Practice

Subtract the fractions and mixed numbers. Simplify your answers when necessary.

1. $15\frac{5}{6}$
   $-\ 9$
   _____
   $6\frac{5}{6}$

2. $8\frac{5}{6}$
   $-\ 3\frac{1}{6}$
   _____

3. $7\frac{9}{24}$
   $-\ 3\frac{6}{24}$
   _____

4. $\frac{5}{6}$
   $-\ \frac{1}{9}$
   _____

5. $\frac{1}{2}$
   $-\ \frac{1}{10}$
   _____

6. $13\frac{11}{15}$
   $-\ 4\frac{2}{5}$
   _____

7. $\frac{1}{3}$
   $-\ \frac{1}{12}$
   _____

8. $7\frac{2}{3}$
   $-\ 4\frac{5}{8}$
   _____

9. $18\frac{3}{4}$
   $-\ 15\frac{7}{12}$
   _____

10. $\frac{9}{10}$
    $-\ \frac{2}{5}$
    _____

11. $8\frac{7}{8}$
    $-\ 6$
    _____

12. $5\frac{5}{6}$
    $-\ \frac{7}{10}$
    _____

Renaming Whole Numbers

Sometimes when you subtract, you must know how to rename a whole number as a mixed number.

Finish the mixed number in each problem.

Whole Number	Mixed Number	

1. $4 \ = \ 3\dfrac{\boxed{4}}{4}$

2. $3 \ = \ 2\dfrac{\boxed{}}{8}$

3. $5 \ = \ 4\dfrac{\boxed{}}{2}$

4. $3 \ = \ 2\dfrac{\boxed{}}{5}$

Mastering the Skill

Rename the whole numbers as mixed numbers.

To rename 4 to $3\frac{3}{3}$ think:

$$4 = 3 + 1$$
$$= 3 + \frac{3}{3}$$
$$= 3\frac{3}{3}$$

To rename 9 to $8\frac{5}{5}$ think:

$$9 = 8 + 1$$
$$= 8 + \frac{5}{5}$$
$$= 8\frac{5}{5}$$

Rename the whole numbers below.

1. $8 = 7\frac{\boxed{}}{3}$

2. $6 = 5\frac{\boxed{}}{8}$

3. $2 = 1\frac{\boxed{}}{9}$

4. $3 = 2\frac{\boxed{}}{6}$

5. $4 = 3\frac{\boxed{}}{7}$

6. $3 = 2\frac{\boxed{}}{4}$

7. $11 = 10\frac{\boxed{}}{5}$

8. $7 = 6\frac{\boxed{}}{9}$

9. $1 = \frac{\boxed{}}{10}$

10. $6 = 5\frac{\boxed{}}{14}$

11. $13 = 12\frac{\boxed{}}{15}$

12. $2 = 1\frac{\boxed{}}{3}$

13. $5 = 4\frac{\boxed{}}{2}$

14. $17 = 16\frac{\boxed{}}{4}$

15. $4 = 3\frac{\boxed{}}{9}$

16. $9 = 8\frac{\boxed{}}{7}$

17. $8 = 7\frac{\boxed{}}{12}$

18. $6 = 5\frac{\boxed{}}{20}$

Rename and Subtract

If there is no fraction on top, you must rename the whole number before you subtract.

<table>
<tr><td></td><td>STEP 1</td><td>STEP 2</td></tr>
</table>

To subtract:

Use a like denominator to rename the whole number.

Subtract the mixed numbers.

$$9 \leftarrow \text{no fraction}$$
$$-\ 6\frac{1}{4}$$

$$9 \quad = \quad 8\frac{4}{4}$$
$$-\ 6\frac{1}{4} = -\ 6\frac{1}{4}$$

like denominators

$$9 \quad = \quad 8\frac{4}{4}$$
$$-\ 6\frac{1}{4} = -\ 6\frac{1}{4}$$
$$\rule{2cm}{0.4pt}$$
$$2\frac{3}{4}$$

Rename the whole numbers and subtract.

1. $6 = 5\frac{\boxed{}}{3}$
   $-\ 2\frac{2}{3} = -2\ \frac{2}{3}$

5. 8
   $-\ 5\frac{7}{10}$

9. 5
   $-\ 1\frac{7}{8}$

2. $4 = 3\frac{\boxed{}}{2}$
   $-\ 3\frac{1}{2} = -\ 3\ \frac{1}{2}$

6. 11
   $-\ 3\frac{11}{12}$

10. 7
   $-\ 3\frac{4}{5}$

3. 8
   $-\ 6\frac{2}{5}$

7. 7
   $-\ \frac{3}{4}$

11. 10
   $-\ 9\frac{1}{8}$

4. 3
   $-\ 1\frac{7}{8}$

8. 10
   $-\ 4\frac{5}{7}$

12. 11
   $-\ 9\frac{1}{4}$

Rename Mixed Numbers

Sometimes when you subtract, you must know how to rename the mixed numbers. Complete the problems by renaming the fractions.

1. $3\frac{1}{4}$ = $2\frac{\boxed{5}}{4}$

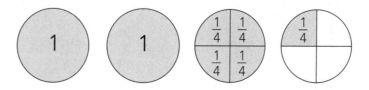

2. $2\frac{1}{3}$ = $1\frac{\boxed{}}{3}$

3. $4\frac{1}{2}$ = $3\frac{\boxed{}}{2}$

4. $3\frac{5}{6}$ = $2\frac{\boxed{}}{6}$

Mixed Number Readiness

To rename $4\frac{1}{3}$ to $3\frac{4}{3}$ think:

$$4\frac{1}{3} = 3 + 1 + \frac{1}{3}$$
$$= 3 + \frac{3}{3} + \frac{1}{3}$$
$$= 3\frac{4}{3}$$

To rename $3\frac{2}{9}$ to $2\frac{11}{9}$ think:

$$3\frac{2}{9} = 2 + 1 + \frac{2}{9}$$
$$= 2 + \frac{9}{9} + \frac{2}{9}$$
$$= 2\frac{11}{9}$$

Rename the mixed numbers.

1. $5\frac{3}{8} = 4\frac{\boxed{}}{8}$

Think:

$$5\frac{3}{8} = 4 + 1 + \frac{3}{8}$$
$$= 4 + \frac{\boxed{}}{8} + \frac{3}{8}$$
$$= 4\,\frac{\boxed{}}{\boxed{}}$$

2. $7\frac{3}{5} = 6\frac{\boxed{}}{5}$

Think:

$$7\frac{3}{5} = 6 + \boxed{} + \frac{\boxed{}}{\boxed{}}$$
$$= 6 + \frac{\boxed{}}{\boxed{}} + \frac{\boxed{}}{\boxed{}}$$
$$= 6\,\frac{\boxed{}}{\boxed{}}$$

3. $4\frac{1}{2} = 3\frac{\boxed{}}{2}$

Think:

$$4\frac{1}{2} = 3 + \boxed{} + \frac{\boxed{}}{\boxed{}}$$
$$= 3 + \frac{\boxed{}}{\boxed{}} + \frac{\boxed{}}{\boxed{}}$$
$$= 3\,\frac{\boxed{}}{\boxed{}}$$

4. $8\frac{2}{3} = 7\frac{\boxed{}}{3}$

Think:

$$8\frac{2}{3} = 7 + \boxed{} + \frac{\boxed{}}{\boxed{}}$$
$$= 7 + \frac{\boxed{}}{\boxed{}} + \frac{\boxed{}}{\boxed{}}$$
$$= 7\,\frac{\boxed{}}{\boxed{}}$$

Fractions: Addition & Subtraction

Renaming Shortcut

Rename $3\frac{3}{4}$.

Take 1 from the whole number and put it in fraction form.

Add the numerators and put the sum over the denominator.

$$3\frac{3}{4} = 2\frac{3}{4} + 1\frac{4}{4}$$

$$2\frac{3+4}{4} = 2\frac{7}{4}$$

Rename the fractions.

1. $6\frac{7}{8} = 5\frac{\square}{8}$

2. $4\frac{5}{9} = 3\frac{\square}{9}$

3. $13\frac{1}{3} = 12\frac{\square}{3}$

4. $9\frac{4}{5} = 8\frac{\square}{5}$

5. $7\frac{5}{6} = 6\frac{\square}{6}$

6. $2\frac{4}{14} = 1\frac{\square}{14}$

7. $7\frac{7}{20} = 6\frac{\square}{20}$

8. $5\frac{7}{18} = 4\frac{\square}{18}$

9. $13\frac{7}{10} = 12\frac{\square}{10}$

10. $19\frac{2}{7} = 18\frac{\square}{7}$

Rename to Subtract

If the fraction to be subtracted is larger than the top fraction, you must rename the top mixed number before you subtract.

	STEP 1	STEP 2	STEP 3
To subtract:	Rename the top mixed number.	Subtract.	Simplify.

$$4\frac{3}{8}$$
$$-\ 1\frac{7}{8} \leftarrow \text{larger numerator}$$

STEP 1 — Rename the top mixed number.

$$4\frac{3}{8} = 3\frac{11}{8}$$
$$-\ 1\frac{7}{8} = -\ 1\frac{7}{8}$$

STEP 2 — Subtract.

$$3\frac{11}{8}$$
$$-\ 1\frac{7}{8}$$
$$\overline{\quad 2\frac{4}{8}}$$

STEP 3 — Simplify.

$$2\frac{4}{8} = 2\frac{1}{2}$$

Rename the top mixed number and subtract. Simplify when necessary.

1. $7\frac{3}{8} = 6-$

   $-\ 4\frac{5}{8} = -\ 4-$

4. $16\frac{4}{6} =$

   $-\ 8\frac{5}{6} =$

7. $3\frac{1}{4} =$

   $-\ 1\frac{3}{4} =$

2. $6\frac{2}{5} = 5-$

   $-\ \frac{4}{5} = -\ -$

5. $7\frac{3}{7} =$

   $-\ 5\frac{6}{7} =$

8. $7\frac{2}{5} =$

   $-\ \frac{3}{5} =$

3. $20\frac{1}{6} =$

   $-\ 15\frac{5}{6} =$

6. $4\frac{4}{10} =$

   $-\ \frac{7}{10} =$

9. $10\frac{4}{9} =$

   $-\ 6\frac{7}{9} =$

Subtract Unlike Mixed Numbers

	STEP 1	STEP 2	STEP 3
To subtract:	Change to the same denominators.	Rename.	Subtract and simplify.

$$5\frac{1}{6}$$
$$-\ 2\frac{2}{3}$$ unlike denominators

STEP 1:
$$5\frac{1}{6} = 5\frac{1}{6}$$
$$-\ 2\frac{2}{3} = -\ 2\frac{4}{6}$$

STEP 2:
$$5\frac{1}{6} = 4\frac{7}{6}$$
$$-\ 2\frac{4}{6} = -\ 2\frac{4}{6}$$

STEP 3:
$$4\frac{7}{6}$$
$$-\ 2\frac{4}{6}$$
$$2\frac{3}{6} = 2\frac{1}{2}$$

Rename and subtract the numbers. Simplify your answers when necessary.

1. $7\frac{1}{4} = 7\frac{}{8} = 6\frac{}{}$
   $-\ 5\frac{3}{8} = 5\frac{}{8} = 5\frac{}{}$

5. $13\frac{1}{3} =$
   $-\ 9\frac{7}{9} =$

2. $5\frac{1}{3} =$
   $-\ 2\frac{5}{6} =$

6. $8\frac{1}{9} =$
   $-\ 3\frac{5}{6} =$

3. $8\frac{7}{10} =$
   $-\ 5\frac{4}{5} =$

7. $9\frac{3}{10} =$
   $-\ 2\frac{1}{2} =$

4. $4\frac{7}{12} =$
   $-\ 2\frac{3}{4} =$

8. $15\frac{1}{3} =$
   $-\ 7\frac{1}{2} =$

Decide to Rename

EXAMPLE 1	EXAMPLE 2	EXAMPLE 3
Rename if there is no fraction on top.	Rename if the smaller fraction is on top.	Find the lowest common denominator (LCD) and rename.

$$6$$
$$-\ 4\frac{3}{8}$$

$$8\frac{2}{7}$$
$$-\ 1\frac{5}{7}$$

$$4\frac{1}{6} = \quad 4\frac{1}{6} = \quad 3\frac{7}{6}$$
$$-\ 2\frac{2}{3} = -\ 2\frac{4}{6} = -\ 2\frac{4}{6}$$

find LCD →   ← rename

Look at each problem carefully. Decide whether or not to rename before you subtract.

1. $6\frac{1}{10} =$
$-\ 1\frac{2}{5} =$

5. $9\frac{1}{3} =$
$-\ 4\frac{5}{6} =$

2. $8\frac{1}{8} =$
$-\ 3\frac{1}{4} =$

6. $13\frac{1}{5} =$
$-\ 6\frac{5}{8} =$

3. $5\frac{1}{2} =$
$-\ 2\frac{5}{6} =$

7. $12\frac{1}{12} =$
$-\ 8\frac{5}{6} =$

4. $13\frac{1}{3} =$
$-\ 4\frac{7}{12} =$

8. $23\frac{1}{6} =$
$-\ 15\frac{7}{10} =$

Mixed Practice

Subtract the mixed numbers and fractions. Simplify your answers when necessary.

1. $\dfrac{7}{8}$
$-\ \dfrac{1}{4}$
_____

5. $9\dfrac{3}{4}$
$-\ 3\dfrac{1}{3}$
_____

9. 16
$-\ 5\dfrac{5}{6}$
_____

2. $9\dfrac{1}{3}$
$-\ 4\dfrac{5}{6}$
_____

6. $9\dfrac{7}{10}$
$-\ 6\dfrac{9}{10}$
_____

10. $8\dfrac{1}{5}$
$-\ 2\dfrac{1}{3}$
_____

3. 8
$-\ 1\dfrac{7}{16}$
_____

7. $14\dfrac{1}{4}$
$-\ 5\dfrac{2}{3}$
_____

11. $1\dfrac{1}{4}$
$-\ \dfrac{5}{6}$
_____

4. $6\dfrac{4}{5}$
$-\ \dfrac{1}{2}$
_____

8. $7\dfrac{2}{3}$
$-\ 3$
_____

12. $\dfrac{5}{6}$
$-\ \dfrac{1}{2}$
_____

Subtraction Review

Subtract the numbers. Simplify the answer when necessary.

1.
$$\frac{7}{13}$$
$$-\frac{5}{13}$$

2.
$$2\frac{5}{11}$$
$$-1\frac{4}{11}$$

3.
$$\frac{3}{4}$$
$$-\frac{1}{6}$$

4.
$$5\frac{2}{3}$$
$$-3\frac{3}{5}$$

5.
$$6\frac{1}{2}$$
$$-\frac{1}{3}$$

Rename the whole number to a mixed number.

6. $7 = 6\dfrac{\square}{4}$

Rename and subtract.

7.
$$4$$
$$-2\frac{3}{5}$$

Rename the mixed number.

8. $2\frac{1}{2} = 1\dfrac{\square}{2}$

Rename and subtract. Simplify the answer when necessary.

9.
$$3\frac{1}{3}$$
$$-1\frac{2}{3}$$

10.
$$9\frac{1}{9}$$
$$-4\frac{5}{6}$$

11.
$$3\frac{1}{8}$$
$$-1\frac{3}{4}$$

12.
$$5$$
$$-2\frac{2}{11}$$

Mixed Addition and Subtraction

Use the signs to decide whether to add or subtract. Simplify answers when necessary.

1. $\begin{array}{r} 3\frac{6}{7} \\ +\ 5\frac{1}{2} \\ \hline \end{array}$

2. $\begin{array}{r} \frac{9}{20} \\ +\ \frac{3}{4} \\ \hline \end{array}$

3. $\begin{array}{r} 16\frac{5}{6} \\ -\ 8\frac{1}{2} \\ \hline \end{array}$

4. $\begin{array}{r} 4\frac{1}{2} \\ +\ 8\frac{7}{10} \\ \hline \end{array}$

5. $\begin{array}{r} 14\frac{1}{4} \\ -\ 6\frac{3}{5} \\ \hline \end{array}$

6. $\begin{array}{r} 21\frac{5}{6} \\ -\ 12\frac{9}{10} \\ \hline \end{array}$

7. $\begin{array}{r} 6\frac{1}{3} \\ +\ 3\frac{1}{6} \\ \hline \end{array}$

8. $\begin{array}{r} \frac{5}{6} \\ -\ \frac{1}{4} \\ \hline \end{array}$

9. $\begin{array}{r} 13\frac{1}{3} \\ -\ 8\frac{5}{6} \\ \hline \end{array}$

10. $\begin{array}{r} 11\frac{11}{12} \\ +\ 5\frac{3}{4} \\ \hline \end{array}$

11. $\begin{array}{r} 28\frac{2}{15} \\ -\ 19\frac{4}{5} \\ \hline \end{array}$

12. $\begin{array}{r} 17\frac{7}{9} \\ +\ 15\frac{5}{6} \\ \hline \end{array}$

Putting It All Together

Number Relation Symbols
$<$ is less than
$>$ is greater than
$=$ is equal to

Place the symbols $<$, $>$, or $=$ in the ◯ to make each problem true.

1. $\dfrac{1}{4} + \dfrac{1}{8}$ ◯ $\dfrac{7}{8} - \dfrac{1}{4}$

2. $2\dfrac{5}{6} - 1\dfrac{1}{3}$ ◯ $\dfrac{3}{4} + \dfrac{3}{4}$

3. $3\dfrac{5}{8} + 5\dfrac{1}{2}$ ◯ $9\dfrac{1}{3} - 1\dfrac{1}{6}$

4. $2\dfrac{5}{6} - 1\dfrac{1}{2}$ ◯ $\dfrac{2}{3} + \dfrac{1}{2}$

5. $5\dfrac{1}{3} + 6\dfrac{1}{6}$ ◯ $25\dfrac{4}{5} - 14\dfrac{3}{4}$

6. $2\dfrac{1}{5} - 1\dfrac{1}{3}$ ◯ $8\dfrac{1}{2} - 6\dfrac{3}{4}$

Subtraction Word Problems

Write a number sentence for each problem below. Then write the answer in the sentence below the problem. Read it and ask yourself, "Does the answer make sense?"

1. A board is $5\frac{1}{2}$ inches wide. If the board is $1\frac{1}{4}$ inches too wide, what size must the board be to fit properly?

_____ _____ _____ = _____
number / operation symbol / number / answer

The board must be _____ inches wide to fit properly.

2. Jill took a nap for $\frac{1}{4}$ of an hour on Monday. She took a nap for $\frac{3}{4}$ of an hour on Tuesday. How much longer was Jill's nap on Tuesday?

_____ _____ _____ = _____
number / operation symbol / number / answer

Jill's nap was _____ of an hour longer on Tuesday.

3. It rained $1\frac{1}{4}$ inches on Friday and $\frac{1}{2}$ of an inch on Saturday. How much more did it rain on Friday than on Saturday?

_____ _____ _____ = _____
number / operation symbol / number / answer

It rained _____ of an inch more on Friday.

4. Mr. Jones bought two chickens. One weighed $4\frac{1}{3}$ pounds and the other weighed $1\frac{1}{2}$ pounds less. How much did the other chicken weigh?

_____ _____ _____ = _____
number / operation symbol / number / answer

The other chicken weighed _____ pounds.

5. $3\frac{3}{4}$ gallons of punch were prepared for the party. If $1\frac{1}{2}$ gallons were left, how much punch was used?

_____ _____ _____ = _____
number / operation symbol / number / answer

_____ gallons of punch were used.

6. Aaron divided a candy bar into 8 equal pieces. He ate $\frac{5}{8}$ of it. How much of the candy bar did he leave?

_____ _____ _____ = _____
number / operation symbol / number / answer

Aaron left _____ of the candy bar.

Writing Number Sentences

Write a number sentence for each problem and solve it.

1. Mrs. Lammon had $15\frac{2}{3}$ yards of material for a dress. She used $4\frac{1}{4}$ yards to make the dress. How much material did she have left?

_____ _____ _____ = _____
number · operation symbol · number · answer

Mrs. Lammon had _____ yards of material left.

2. Yesterday Mr. Grasso ran $7\frac{1}{2}$ miles. Today he ran $4\frac{3}{4}$ miles. How much farther did he run yesterday?

_____ _____ _____ = _____
number · operation symbol · number · answer

Mr. Grasso ran _____ miles farther yesterday.

3. Victoria bought $3\frac{1}{2}$ yards of cloth. She used $1\frac{1}{4}$ yards to make a skirt. How many yards of cloth does she have left?

_____ _____ _____ = _____
number · operation symbol · number · answer

Victoria has _____ yards of cloth left.

4. Mr. Yao had $3\frac{1}{3}$ gallons of gas in his car. He filled up his $20\frac{1}{2}$-gallon tank. How much gas did he buy to fill the tank?

_____ _____ _____ = _____
number · operation symbol · number · answer

Mr. Yao bought _____ gallons of gas.

5. Tola used $1\frac{1}{3}$ cups of sugar and $\frac{3}{4}$ cup of milk in a recipe. How much more sugar was used than milk?

_____ _____ _____ = _____
number · operation symbol · number · answer

Tola used _____ cup(s) more sugar.

6. A baby weighed $6\frac{3}{8}$ pounds at birth. After three weeks the baby weighed $8\frac{1}{2}$ pounds. How many pounds did the baby gain?

_____ _____ _____ = _____
number · operation symbol · number · answer

The baby gained _____ pounds.

Use Drawings to Solve Problems

Seeing a picture or drawing a picture may help you solve problems.

How far is it from Delta to Franklin?

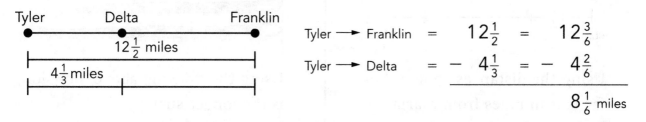

Use the pictures to solve the problems.

1. How far is it from Redford to Rover? _____

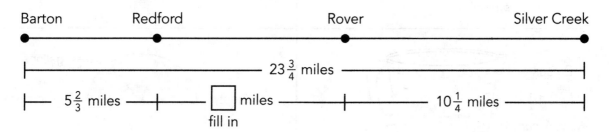

2. Fill in: Pearl to Colon is $7\frac{1}{2}$ miles. Union to Colon is $29\frac{1}{4}$ miles.

    How far is it from Union to Pearl? _____

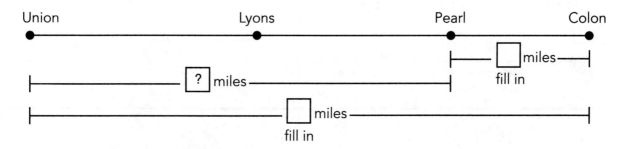

3. Sketch a drawing on the line below to help solve the problem.

    Leslie is between Evart and Owosso.

    Evart to Leslie is $8\frac{1}{2}$ miles.

    Evart to Owosso is $11\frac{3}{4}$ miles.

    How far is it from Leslie to Owosso? _____

Picture Problems

Use the drawings to help solve the addition and subtraction problems.

1.

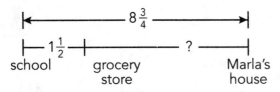

school   grocery store   Marla's house

Using the distances shown, how far is it in miles from Marla's house to the grocery store?

_____ _____ _____ = _____
operation symbol   answer

2.

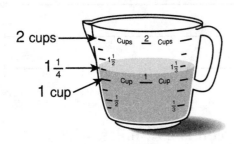

2 cups

$1\frac{1}{4}$

1 cup

Using the measuring cup, how much more is needed to make 2 cups?

_____ _____ _____ = _____
operation symbol   answer

3.

The shaded pieces represent pieces of pie already eaten. How much of the pie will be gone if $\frac{1}{4}$ more is eaten?

_____ _____ _____ = _____
operation symbol   answer

4.

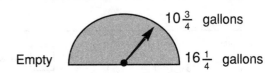

$3\frac{1}{3}$ feet $\frac{3}{4}$ foot

Using the drawing above, how long is the longer snake?

_____ _____ _____ = _____
operation symbol   answer

5.

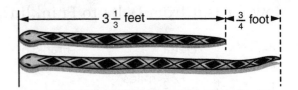

$10\frac{3}{4}$ gallons

Empty $16\frac{1}{4}$ gallons

Using the drawing above, how many gallons of gas did Adam use if the tank was full to begin with?

_____ _____ _____ = _____
operation symbol   answer

6.

$13\frac{1}{2}$ inches

Using the drawing above, how long is Sarah's hair now if it has grown $2\frac{3}{4}$ inches?

_____ _____ _____ = _____
operation symbol   answer

Add or Subtract

When you read a word problem, you have to decide what operation to use.

You **add** when you:
• Combine
• Find a total
• Join together

You **subtract** when you:
• Find a difference
• Take away
• Find what is less

Mr. Emilio drove $7\frac{3}{4}$ hours on Monday and $5\frac{1}{2}$ hours on Tuesday. How many hours did he travel in all?

$$7\frac{3}{4} = 7\frac{6}{8}$$
$$+\ 5\frac{1}{2} = +5\frac{4}{8}$$
$$\overline{\qquad\qquad 12\frac{10}{8} = 13\frac{2}{8} = 13\frac{1}{4} \text{ hours}}$$

Virgil bought $9\frac{3}{4}$ gallons of gas on Friday and $5\frac{5}{8}$ gallons of gas on Monday. How much more gas did Virgil buy on Friday?

$$9\frac{3}{4} = 9\frac{6}{8}$$
$$-\ 5\frac{5}{8} = -5\frac{5}{8}$$
$$\overline{\qquad\qquad 4\frac{1}{8} \text{ gallons}}$$

Carefully read the problems below. Decide whether to add or subtract. Then solve the problem.

1. Mark watched television $1\frac{1}{2}$ hours before dinner and $2\frac{1}{3}$ hours after dinner. How long did he watch television?

   _____ _____ _____ = _____
   operation   answer
   symbol

   Mark watched television _____ hours in all.

2. Lester cut $2\frac{3}{8}$ inches off a 12-inch pipe. How long is the remaining piece?

   _____ _____ _____ = _____
   operation   answer
   symbol

   The remaining piece is _____ inches long.

3. Andrea worked $7\frac{3}{4}$ hours on Wednesday and 12 hours on Thursday. How many more hours did she work on Thursday?

   _____ _____ _____ = _____
   operation   answer
   symbol

   Andrea worked _____ hours longer on Thursday.

4. A carpenter drew a line segment $6\frac{1}{2}$ inches long. He then extended it another $\frac{13}{16}$ of an inch. How long was the line segment?

   _____ _____ _____ = _____
   operation   answer
   symbol

   The line segment was _____ inches long.

Using Symbols

Joel practiced $\frac{3}{4}$ of an hour on Monday and 2 hours on Tuesday. Using these facts, fill in the blanks below.

1. Joel practiced $1\frac{1}{4}$ hours longer on Tuesday than on Monday.

$$\frac{3}{4} \quad + \quad \underline{\hspace{1cm}} \quad = \quad 2$$
Monday   answer   Tuesday

2. Joel practiced $1\frac{1}{4}$ hours less on Monday than on Tuesday

$$2 \quad - \quad \underline{\hspace{1cm}} \quad = \quad \frac{3}{4}$$
Tuesday   answer   Monday

3. Tuesday's practice was greater (longer) than Monday's.

$$\underline{\hspace{1cm}} \quad > \quad \underline{\hspace{1cm}}$$
Tuesday   Monday

4. Monday's practice was less (shorter) than Tuesday's.

$$\underline{\hspace{1cm}} \quad < \quad \underline{\hspace{1cm}}$$
Monday   Tuesday

5. Joel practiced for different amounts of time.

$$\frac{3}{4} \quad \underline{\hspace{1cm}} \quad 2$$
Monday   symbol   Tuesday

Anna drew a line segment $5\frac{1}{4}$ inches long. Sue drew a line segment $2\frac{1}{2}$ inches long. Using these facts, fill in the blanks below.

6. Anna's line segment is $2\frac{3}{4}$ inches longer than Sue's.

$$2\frac{1}{2} \quad + \quad \underline{\hspace{1cm}} \quad = \quad 5\frac{1}{4}$$
Sue   answer   Anna

7. Sue's line segment is $2\frac{3}{4}$ inches less (shorter) than Anna's.

$$5\frac{1}{4} \quad - \quad \underline{\hspace{1cm}} \quad = \quad 2\frac{1}{2}$$
Anna   answer   Sue

8. Anna drew a longer line segment than Sue.

$$\underline{\hspace{1cm}} \quad > \quad \underline{\hspace{1cm}}$$
Anna   Sue

9. Sue drew a shorter line segment than Anna.

$$\underline{\hspace{1cm}} \quad < \quad \underline{\hspace{1cm}}$$
Sue   Anna

10. Anna and Sue drew line segments of different lengths.

$$5\frac{1}{4} \quad \underline{\hspace{1cm}} \quad 2\frac{1}{2}$$
Anna   symbol   Sue

Write a Question

To decide whether to add or subtract, you must read carefully. One way to learn to read carefully is to write your own questions.

1. Two boards measure $6\frac{3}{8}$ feet and $3\frac{1}{4}$ feet.

   Write a question about the facts if the answer is:

   a) $9\frac{5}{8}$ How long are the boards altogether?

   b) $3\frac{1}{8}$ _____

4. Carlos cut $\frac{7}{8}$ inch off a 5-inch board. Ed cut $\frac{1}{2}$ inch off a 7-inch board.

   Write a question about the facts if the answer is:

   a) $4\frac{1}{8}$ _____

   b) $6\frac{1}{2}$ _____

2. Sarah bought $3\frac{1}{2}$ pounds of ham, $1\frac{1}{4}$ pounds of beef, and $2\frac{3}{4}$ pounds of fish.

   Write a question about the facts if the answer is:

   a) $\frac{3}{4}$ How much more ham than fish did she buy?

   b) $2\frac{1}{4}$ _____

5. Serena bought $2\frac{1}{4}$ pounds of candy and $1\frac{1}{2}$ pounds of peanuts.

   Write a question about the facts if the answer is:

   a) $\frac{3}{4}$ _____

   b) $3\frac{3}{4}$ _____

3. A carpenter drew line segments of $3\frac{1}{2}$ inches and $1\frac{1}{3}$ inches.

   Write a question about the facts if the answer is:

   a) $2\frac{1}{6}$ _____

   b) $4\frac{5}{6}$ _____

6. It takes $1\frac{1}{4}$ hours by plane, $2\frac{1}{2}$ hours by train, and 4 hours by car.

   Write a question about the facts if the answer is:

   a) $2\frac{3}{4}$ _____

   b) $1\frac{1}{2}$ _____

Decide to Add or Subtract

1. Read the facts carefully.

2. Decide whether to write an addition or subtraction question.

3. Write a question and a number sentence.

4. Compare your answer with the question. Ask yourself. "Does the answer make sense?"

---

1. Linda worked $2\frac{1}{5}$ hours of overtime on Monday and $3\frac{1}{2}$ hours of overtime on Tuesday.

Question: <u>How many hours of</u> <u>overtime did she work in all?</u>

_____ $+$ _____ $=$ _____
operation   answer
symbol

4. A board is 60 inches long and $5\frac{1}{4}$ inches must be cut off.

Question: _____

_____

_____ _____ _____ $=$ _____
operation   answer
symbol

---

2. The recipe called for $\frac{1}{4}$ pound of peanuts and $\frac{1}{2}$ pound of chocolate chips.

Question: _____

_____

_____ _____ _____ $=$ _____
operation   answer
symbol

5. Mr. Miller drove $\frac{1}{2}$ of the way the first day and $\frac{1}{3}$ of the way the second day.

Question: _____

_____

_____ _____ _____ $=$ _____
operation   answer
symbol

---

3. Paul drove $25\frac{5}{6}$ miles north and $6\frac{1}{2}$ miles east from his house to Brad's house.

Question: _____

_____

_____ _____ _____ $=$ _____
operation   answer
symbol

6.

|←——————$15\frac{1}{2}$——————→|

|←—$3\frac{1}{3}$—|————— ? ——→|
home   school   store

Question: _____

_____

_____ _____ _____ $=$ _____
operation   answer
symbol

Mixed Problem-Solving Review

Decide whether to add or subtract. Write a number sentence and fill in the answer below. Ask yourself, "Does the answer make sense?"

1. On Monday the fuel gauge read $\frac{7}{8}$ full. On Friday the fuel gauge read $\frac{1}{4}$ full. What is the difference in readings?

    _____ _____ _____ = _____
           operation   answer
           symbol

    The difference in readings is _____ .

2. Kris nailed a $4\frac{5}{8}$-foot board next to a $7\frac{9}{16}$-foot board. What is the total length of both boards?

    _____ _____ _____ = _____
           operation   answer
           symbol

    The total length of both boards is _____ feet.

3. Last month it rained $2\frac{3}{8}$ inches. This month it has rained $1\frac{1}{3}$ inches. How much more rain fell last month?

    _____ _____ _____ = _____
           operation   answer
           symbol

    It rained _____ inches more last month.

4. Grover bought 4 gallons of paint to paint his house. If he has used $2\frac{1}{8}$ gallons, how much does he have left?

    _____ _____ _____ = _____
           operation   answer
           symbol

    Grover has _____ gallons of paint left.

5. A bread recipe calls for $1\frac{1}{2}$ cups of flour and $\frac{1}{4}$ cup of bran. How many cups of these ingredients are there in all?

    _____ _____ _____ = _____
           operation   answer
           symbol

    There are _____ cups of these ingredients in all.

6. Nora bought $1\frac{1}{3}$ pounds of candy and $\frac{3}{5}$ pound of peanuts. How many pounds did she buy?

    _____ _____ _____ = _____
           operation   answer
           symbol

    Nora bought _____ pounds.

Weighing Food

Food is sometimes measured in pounds.

This scale hold up to ___4___ pounds.

The arrow is pointing to ___$2\frac{1}{2}$___ pounds.

A. Label the $\frac{1}{4}$ and $\frac{3}{4}$ pound marks for each pound.

Use the scales to answer the questions.

1. a) This scale holds up to _____ pounds.

b) What letter is on the $1\frac{3}{4}$ pound mark? _____

c) How much does the food weigh? _____

d) If you remove $\frac{3}{4}$ pound of the food, how much will the remaining food weigh? _____

2. If you remove $\frac{3}{8}$ pound of food, how much will the remaining food weigh? _____

3. How many pounds does Scott need to add to make 6 pounds? _____

Reading a Measuring Cup

A. Fill in the measurements next to the correct lines.

$\frac{1}{2}$, $\frac{2}{3}$, $\frac{3}{4}$, $1\frac{1}{4}$, $1\frac{1}{3}$, $1\frac{1}{2}$

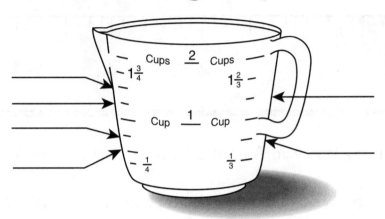

---

1. On the drawings below, shade in the amounts listed.

a) $\frac{3}{4}$ cup **b)** $\frac{1}{3}$ cup **c)** $\frac{2}{3}$ cup **d)** $\frac{1}{2}$ cup

2. 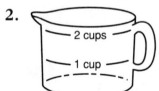 Jack needs 3 cups of flour to make bread. How many times will he need to fill up this measuring cup? _____

3. Jane is making tuna salad. Fill in the blanks to indicate the amount shown in each picture.

onions   relish   tuna fish   mayonnaise

a) _____   **b)** _____   **c)** _____   **d)** _____

Math for the Carpenter

1. a) Write an A on the $1\frac{1}{2}$ inch mark.

b) Write a B on the $3\frac{1}{8}$ inch mark.

c) Write a C on the $\frac{3}{4}$ inch mark.

d) Write a D on the $5\frac{3}{8}$ inch mark.

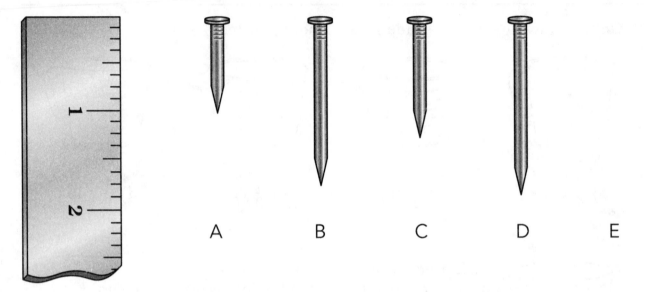

A   B   C   D   E

2. a) How long is nail A? _____

b) How long is nail D? _____

3. Jason needs a nail longer than 1 inch but shorter than $1\frac{1}{2}$ inches. Which of the nails above should he use?

4. Next to nail D, draw nail E 2 inches long.

    Fractions: Addition & Subtraction

Fractions of an Hour

Hands move this way

$\frac{1}{4}$	hour =	15 minutes
$\frac{1}{2}$	hour =	30 minutes
$\frac{3}{4}$	hour =	45 minutes
1	hour =	60 minutes

Use the clock and information box above to help answer the questions.

1. 1 hour and 30 minutes = __$1\frac{1}{2}$__ hours.

2. What time is shown on the clock? _____

3. a) $\frac{1}{4}$ hour = _____ minutes.

   b) What time will the clock read in $\frac{1}{4}$ of an hour? _____

4. A quarter past 12 = _____

5. It's 1:30. Maggie has an appointment in half an hour.

   a) How many minutes does she have before her appointment? _____

   b) What time is her appointment? _____

6. It's 1:30. How long is it until 5 o'clock? Write a mixed number. _____

Using Road Signs

Find the "X" in the drawing. This shows you where each road sign is located. Use the distances given in the drawing and on the large road sign to find each missing distance.

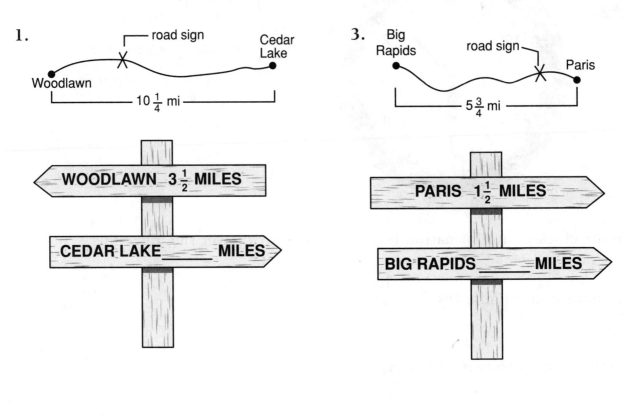

1. road sign — Cedar Lake — Woodlawn — 10 ¼ mi

WOODLAWN 3½ MILES

CEDAR LAKE ____ MILES

3. Big Rapids — road sign — Paris — 5¾ mi

PARIS 1½ MILES

BIG RAPIDS ____ MILES

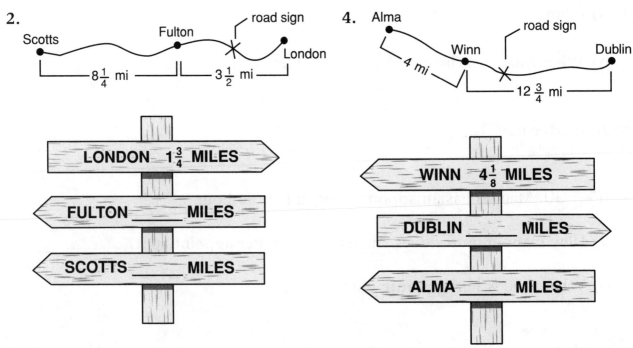

2. Scotts — Fulton — road sign — London — 8¼ mi — 3½ mi

LONDON 1¾ MILES

FULTON ____ MILES

SCOTTS ____ MILES

4. Alma — Winn — road sign — Dublin — 4 mi — 12¾ mi

WINN 4⅛ MILES

DUBLIN ____ MILES

ALMA ____ MILES

Apply Your Skills

1. Reinhardt bought $1\frac{2}{3}$ pounds of grapes, $3\frac{3}{4}$ pounds of apples, and $2\frac{1}{3}$ pounds of oranges. How many pounds did he buy in all?

    Answer: _____

2. Pierre used $1\frac{3}{4}$ cups of sugar and $\frac{1}{3}$ cup of brown sugar to make cookies. How much sugar did he use in all?

    Answer: _____

3. It is 11:45. Mr. Suarez has a meeting in 45 minutes. What time is his meeting?

    Answer: _____

4. At 2:30, Christine realized that her appointment is in 90 minutes. What time is her appointment?

    Answer: _____

5. It is 3:15. How long is it until 7:00? Write a mixed number.

    Answer: _____

6. Emily drove $35\frac{1}{2}$ miles on Monday and $44\frac{2}{3}$ miles on Tuesday. How far did she drive on both days?

    Answer: _____

7. It is 178 miles from Chicago to Ripon. Amy has driven $76\frac{3}{4}$ miles. How much farther does she have to drive?

    Answer: _____

8. Carolyn plays tennis at 2:30. It will take her 45 minutes to get there. What time should she leave?

    Answer: _____

Life-Skills Math Review

1. How many pounds does Lilla need to add to make 5 pounds?

Answer: _____

2. Shade in $\frac{2}{3}$ cup.

Answer: _____

3. How much liquid is in this cup?

Answer: _____

4. How many gallons are needed to fill the tank?

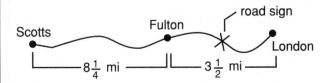

9$\frac{1}{2}$ gallons

Empty

16$\frac{1}{4}$ gallons

Answer: _____

5. It is 11:45 and Joann has an appointment in $\frac{3}{4}$ of an hour.

   a) How many minutes does she have before her appointment?

   Answer: _____

   b) What time is her appointment?

   Answer: _____

6. It is now 2:15. How long is it until 7 o'clock? Write a mixed number.

Answer: _____

7. How far is it from Scotts to London?

Scotts   Fulton   road sign   London

8$\frac{1}{4}$ mi   3$\frac{1}{2}$ mi

Answer: _____

8. It is is $3\frac{3}{4}$ miles from Woodlawn to the road sign. How far is it from the road sign to Cedar Lake?

road sign   Cedar Lake

Woodlawn

10$\frac{1}{4}$ mi

Answer: _____

Add the fractions. Simplify when necessary.

1. $\dfrac{4}{7}$
   $+ \dfrac{3}{7}$
   _____

2. $\dfrac{10}{4}$
   $+ \dfrac{3}{8}$
   _____

3. $3\dfrac{7}{14}$
   $+ \ 5\dfrac{3}{7}$
   _____

4. $16\dfrac{7}{10}$
   $+ \ 3\dfrac{1}{2}$
   _____

5. $3\dfrac{1}{4}$
   $4\dfrac{3}{8}$
   $+ \ 7\dfrac{1}{2}$
   _____

Subtract the fractions. Simplify when necessary.

6. $\dfrac{15}{17}$
   $- \dfrac{4}{17}$
   _____

7. $\dfrac{3}{4}$
   $- \dfrac{5}{12}$
   _____

8. $\dfrac{5}{6}$
   $- \dfrac{1}{12}$
   _____

9. $16\dfrac{1}{2}$
   $- \ 8\dfrac{5}{6}$
   _____

10. $21\dfrac{2}{15}$
    $- \ 19\dfrac{4}{5}$
    _____

Simplify each answer.

1. $\dfrac{1}{6}$

$+ \dfrac{2}{3}$

Answer: _____

6. Simplify $5\dfrac{9}{4}$.

Answer: _____

2. It takes $2\dfrac{1}{4}$ hours to travel from Kalamazoo to Detroit by train. It takes $\dfrac{1}{2}$ hour to fly. How much longer does it take by train?

Answer: _____

7. $\dfrac{1}{2}$

$- \dfrac{3}{8}$

Answer: _____

3. $7\dfrac{1}{5}$

$+ 3\dfrac{2}{3}$

Answer: _____

8. Bob is on a 60-mile bicycle tour. He rode $28\dfrac{3}{10}$ miles and then stopped to eat lunch. How much farther did he have to ride after lunch?

Answer: _____

4. A repairman made two service calls. He spent $2\dfrac{1}{4}$ hours on the first call and $1\dfrac{1}{2}$ hours on the other. How many hours did he spend on the service calls altogether?

Answer: _____

9. A tabletop is $2\dfrac{3}{8}$ inches thick. It sits on legs that are $27\dfrac{5}{16}$ inches high. What is the combined height of the tabletop and the legs?

Answer: _____

5. $12 - 8\dfrac{5}{6} =$

Answer: _____

10. $9\dfrac{3}{4}$

$- 3\dfrac{1}{3}$

Answer: _____

11. $4\frac{5}{6} + 9\frac{1}{6} =$

Answer: _____

16. The town of Greenport needs to raise $2 million to build a new gym and pool. So far they have raised $1\frac{1}{4}$ million. How much more money do they need?

Answer: _____

12. The mixed number $9\frac{7}{12}$ is equal to 8 and how many twelfths?

Answer: _____

17. Steve spent $4\frac{3}{4}$ hours painting his garage, and his son Jed spent $2\frac{1}{2}$ hours helping him. Together how many hours did it take them to paint the garage?

Answer: _____

13. $3\frac{1}{2} + 2\frac{3}{4} + 5\frac{3}{8} =$

Answer: _____

18. $4\frac{5}{8} - 1\frac{3}{4} =$

Answer: _____

14. $7\frac{1}{6}$
  $-\ 4\frac{1}{3}$
  _____

Answer: _____

19. Joan bought $4\frac{3}{16}$ pounds of ground beef and $3\frac{3}{4}$ pounds of chicken. What was the total weight of the meat that she bought?

Answer: _____

15. $\frac{1}{3}$
  $\frac{5}{8}$
  $+\ \frac{1}{4}$
  _____

Answer: _____

20. Eric drove $12\frac{3}{8}$ miles on Friday and $25\frac{1}{2}$ miles on Saturday. How many more miles did Eric drive on Saturday?

Answer: _____

Evaluation Chart

On the following chart, circle the number of any problem you missed. The column after the problem number tells you the pages where those problems are taught. You should review the sections for any problems you missed.

Skill Area	Posttest Problem Number	Skill Section	Review Page
Addition	1, 3, 6, 11, 13, 15	7–30	18, 31, 57, 58
Subtraction	5, 7, 10, 12, 14, 18	39–55	56, 57, 58
Addition Problem Solving	4, 9, 17, 19	32–37	38, 66, 67
Subtraction Problem Solving	2, 8, 16, 20	59–65	66, 67
Life-Skills Math	All	68–73	74